THE POETRY OF
RAINER MARIA RILKE

Translated into English with Commentary by

A. S. KLINE

POETRY IN TRANSLATION

www.poetryintranslation.com

CONTENTS

THE DUINO ELEGIES

The Earth, Auguste Rodin（French, 1840 – 1917）
The Getty Open Content Program

THE FIRST ELEGY

Who, if I cried out, would hear me among the Angelic
Orders? And even if one were to suddenly
take me to its heart, I would vanish into its
stronger existence. For beauty is nothing but
the beginning of terror, that we are still able to bear,
and we revere it so, because it calmly disdains
to destroy us. Every Angel is terror.
And so I hold myself back and swallow the cry
of a darkened sobbing. Ah, who then can
we make use of? Not Angels: not men,
and the resourceful creatures see clearly
that we are not really at home
in the interpreted world. Perhaps there remains
some tree on a slope, that we can see
again each day: there remains to us yesterday's street,
and the thinned-out loyalty of a habit
that liked us, and so stayed, and never departed.
Oh, and the night, the night, when the wind full of space
wears out our faces – whom would she not stay for,
the longed-for, gentle, disappointing one, whom the solitary heart
with difficulty stands before. Is she less heavy for lovers?
Ah, they only hide their fate between themselves.
Do you not know yet? Throw the emptiness out of your arms
to add to the spaces we breathe; maybe the birds
will feel the expansion of air, in more intimate flight.

The Cry, Auguste Rodin (French, 1840 – 1917)
The Los Angeles County Museum of Art

Yes, the Spring-times needed you deeply. Many a star

must have been there for you so you might feel it. A wave

lifted towards you out of the past, or, as you walked

past an open window, a violin

gave of itself. All this was their mission.

But could you handle it? Were you not always,

still, distracted by expectation, as if all you experienced,

like a Beloved, came near to you? (Where could you contain her,

with all the vast strange thoughts in you

going in and out, and often staying the night.)

But if you are yearning, then sing the lovers: for long

their notorious feelings have not been immortal enough.

Those, you almost envied them, the forsaken, that you

found as loving as those who were satisfied. Begin,

always as new, the unattainable praising:

think: the hero prolongs himself, even his falling

was only a pretext for being, his latest rebirth.

But lovers are taken back by exhausted Nature

into herself, as if there were not the power

to make them again. Have you remembered

Gastara Stampa [p. 220] sufficiently yet, that any girl,

whose lover has gone, might feel from that

intenser example of love: 'Could I only become like her?'

Should not these ancient sufferings be finally

fruitful for us? Isn't it time that, loving,

we freed ourselves from the beloved, and, trembling, endured

as the arrow endures the bow, so as to be, in its flight,

something more than itself? For staying is nowhere.

Voices, voices. Hear then, my heart, as only
saints have heard: so that the mighty call
raised them from the earth: they, though, knelt on
impossibly and paid no attention:
such was their listening. Not that you could withstand
God's voice: far from it. But listen to the breath,
the unbroken message that creates itself from the silence.
It rushes towards you now, from those youthfully dead.
Whenever you entered, didn't their fate speak to you,
quietly, in churches in Naples or Rome?
Or else an inscription exaltedly impressed itself on you,
as lately the tablet in *Santa Maria Formosa* [p. 220].
What do they will of me? That I should gently remove
the semblance of injustice, that slightly, at times,
hinders their spirits from a pure moving-on.

It is truly strange to no longer inhabit the earth,
to no longer practice customs barely acquired,
not to give a meaning of human futurity
to roses, and other expressly promising things:
no longer to be what one was in endlessly anxious hands,
and to set aside even one's own
proper name like a broken plaything.
Strange: not to go on wishing one's wishes. Strange
to see all that was once in place, floating
so loosely in space. And it's hard being dead,
and full of retrieval, before one gradually feels
a little eternity. Though the living
all make the error of drawing too sharp a distinction.
Angels (they say) would often not know whether
they moved among living or dead. The eternal current
sweeps all the ages, within it, through both the spheres,
forever, and resounds above them in both.

Finally they have no more need of us, the early-departed,
weaned gently from earthly things, as one outgrows
the mother's mild breast. But we, needing
such great secrets, for whom sadness is often
the source of a blessed progress, could we exist without them?
Is it a meaningless story how once, in the grieving for *Linos* [p. 220],
first music ventured to penetrate arid rigidity,
so that, in startled space, which an almost godlike youth
suddenly left forever, the emptiness first felt
the quivering that now enraptures us, and comforts, and helps.

THE SECOND ELEGY

E very Angel is terror. And yet,
ah, knowing you, I invoke you, almost deadly
birds of the soul. Where are the days of *Tobias* [p. 220],
when one of the most radiant of you stood at the simple threshold,
disguised somewhat for the journey and already no longer awesome
(Like a youth, to the youth looking out curiously).
Let the *Archangel* [p. 220] now, the dangerous one, from behind the stars,
take a single step down and toward us: our own heart,
beating on high would beat us down. What are you?

Early successes, Creation's favourite ones,
mountain-chains, ridges reddened by dawns
of all origin – pollen of flowering godhead,
junctions of light, corridors, stairs, thrones,
spaces of being, shields of bliss, tempests
of storm-filled, delighted feeling and, suddenly, solitary
mirrors: gathering their own out-streamed beauty
back into their faces again.

For we, when we feel, evaporate: oh, we
breathe ourselves out and away: from ember to ember,
yielding us fainter fragrance. Then someone may say to us:
'Yes, you are in my blood, the room, the Spring-time
is filling with you'..... What use is that: they cannot hold us,
we vanish inside and around them. And those who are beautiful,
oh, who holds them back? Appearance, endlessly, stands up,
in their face, and goes by. Like dew from the morning grass,
what is ours rises from us, like the heat
from a dish that is warmed. O smile: where? O upward gaze:
new, warm, vanishing wave of the heart - :
oh, we are that. Does the cosmic space,
we dissolve into, taste of us then? Do the Angels
really only take back what is theirs, what has streamed out of them,
or is there sometimes, as if by an oversight, something
of our being, as well? Are we as mingled with their
features, as there is vagueness in the faces
of pregnant women? They do not see it in the swirling
return to themselves. (How should they see it?)

Lovers, if they knew how, might utter
strange things in night air. Since it seems
everything hides us. Look, trees exist; houses,
we live in, still stand. Only we
pass everything by, like an exchange of air.
And all is at one, in keeping us secret, half out of
shame perhaps, half out of inexpressible hope.

Lovers, each satisfied in the other, I ask
you about us. You grasp yourselves. Have you a sign?
Look, it happens to me, that at times my hands
become aware of each other, or that my worn face
hides itself in them. That gives me a slight
sensation. But who would dare to exist only for that?
You, though, who grow in the other's delight
until, overwhelmed, they beg:
'No more' -: you, who under your hands
grow richer like vintage years of the vine:
who sometimes vanish, because the other
has so gained the ascendancy: I ask you of us. I know
you touch so blissfully because the caress withholds,
because the place you cover so tenderly
does not disappear: because beneath it you feel
pure duration. So that you promise eternity
almost, from the embrace. And yet, when you've endured
the first terrible glances, and the yearning at windows,
and the first walk together, just once, through the garden:
Lovers, are you the same? When you raise yourselves
one to another's mouth, and hang there – sip against sip:
O, how strangely the drinker then escapes from their action.

Eternal Idol, Auguste Rodin (French, 1840 – 1917)
The Los Angeles County Museum of Art

Weren't you amazed by the caution of human gesture
on Attic steles? Weren't love and departure
laid so lightly on shoulders, they seemed to be made
of other matter than ours? Think of the hands
how they rest without weight, though there is power in the torso.
Those self-controlled ones know, through that: so much is ours,
this is us, to touch our own selves so: the gods
may bear down more heavily on us. But that is the gods' affair.
If only we too could discover a pure, contained
human place, a strip of fruitful land of our own,
between river and stone! For our own heart exceeds us,
even as theirs did. And we can no longer
gaze after it into images, that soothe it, or into
godlike bodies, where it restrains itself more completely.

THE THIRD ELEGY

To sing the beloved is one thing, another, oh,
that hidden guilty river-god of the blood.
What does he know, himself, of that lord of desire, her young lover,
whom she knows distantly, who often out of his solitariness,
before the girl soothed him, often, as if she did not exist,
held up, dripping, from what unknowable depths,
his godhead, oh, rousing the night to endless uproar?
O Neptune of the blood, O his trident of terrors.
O the dark storm-wind from his chest, out of the twisted conch.
Hear, how the night becomes thinned-out and hollow. You, stars,
is it not from you that the lover's joy in the beloved's
face rises? Does he not gain his innermost insight,
into her face's purity, from the pure stars?

It was not you, alas, not his mother
that bent the arc of his brow into such expectation.
Not for you, girl, feeling his presence, not for you,
did his lips curve into a more fruitful expression.
Do you truly think that your light entrance
rocked him so, you who wander like winds at dawn?
You terrified his heart, that's so: but more ancient terrors
plunged into him with the impetus of touching.
Call him...you can't quite call him away from that dark companion.
Of course he wants to, and does, escape: relieved, winning
his way into your secret heart, and takes on, and begins himself.
Did he ever begin himself, though?
Mother you made his littleness: you were the one who began him:
to you he was new, you hung the friendly world
over new eyes, and defended him from what was strange.
Oh where are the years when you simply repelled
the surging void for him, with your slight form?
You hid so much from him then: you made the suspect room
harmless at night, from your heart filled with refuge
mixed a more human space with his spaces of night.
Not in the darkness, no, in your nearer being
you placed the light, and it shone as if out of friendship.
There wasn't a single creaking you couldn't explain with a smile,
as if you had long known when the floor would do so....
And he heard you and was soothed. Your being
was so tenderly potent: his fate there stepped,
tall and cloaked, behind the wardrobe, and his restless future,
so easily delayed, fitted the folds of the curtain.

Woman and Child, Auguste Rodin (French, 1840 – 1917)
The National Gallery of Art

And he himself, as he lay there, relieved,

dissolving a sweetness, of your gentle creation,

under his sleepy eyelids, into the sleep he had tasted - :

seemed protected.....But inside: who could hinder,

prevent, the primal flood inside him?

Ah, there was little caution in the sleeper: sleeping,

but dreaming, but fevered: what began there!

How, new, fearful, he was tangled

in ever-spreading tendrils of inner event:

already twisted in patterns, in strangling growths,

among prowling bestial forms. How he gave himself to it -. Loved.

Loved his inward world, his inner wilderness,

that first world within, on whose mute overthrow

his heart stood, newly green. Loved. Relinquished it, went on,

through his own roots, to the vast fountain

where his little birth was already outlived. Lovingly

went down into more ancient bloodstreams, into ravines

where Horror lay, still gorged on his forefathers. And every

Terror knew him, winked, like an informant.

Yes, Dread smiled.........Seldom

have you smiled so tenderly, mothers. How could he

help loving what smiled at him. Before you

he loved it, since, while you carried him,

it was dissolved in the waters, that render the embryo light.

See, we don't love like flowers, in a
single year: when we love, an ancient
sap rises in our arms. O, girls,
this: that we loved inside us, not one to come, but
the immeasurable seething: not a single child,
but the fathers: resting on our depths
like the rubble of mountains: the dry river-beds
of those who were mothers - : the whole
silent landscape under a clouded or
clear destiny - : girls, this came before you.

And you yourself, how could you know – that you
stirred up primordial time in your lover. What feelings
welled up from lost lives. What
women hated you there. What sinister men
you roused up in his young veins. Dead
children wanted you.....O, gently, gently,
show him with love a confident daily task - lead him
near to the Garden, give him what outweighs
those nights........
           Be in him...............

THE FOURTH ELEGY

O trees of life, O when are you wintering?
We are not unified. We have no instincts
like those of migratory birds. Useless, and late,
we force ourselves, suddenly, onto the wind,
and fall down to an indifferent lake.
We realise flowering and fading together.
And somewhere lions still roam. Never knowing,
as long as they have their splendour, of any weakness.

We, though, while we are intent on one thing, wholly,
feel the loss of some other. Enmity
is our neighbour. Aren't lovers
always arriving at boundaries, each of the other,
who promised distance, hunting, and home?
And when, for the sketch of a moment,
a contrasting background is carefully prepared
so that we can see it: then this is clear
to us. We do not know the contours
of feeling, only what forms it from outside.
Who has not sat, scared, before his heart's curtain?
It drew itself up: the scenery was of Departure.
Easy to comprehend. The familiar garden
swaying a little: then the dancer appeared.
Not him. Enough! However lightly he moves
he is in costume, and turns into a citizen,
and goes through the kitchen into his house.
I don't want these half-completed masks,
rather the Doll. That is complete. I will

suffer its shell, its wire, its face
of mere appearance. Here. I am waiting.
Even if the lights go out, even if someone
says to me: 'No more' - , even if emptiness
reaches me as a grey draught of air from the stage,
even if none of my silent forefathers
sits by me any more, not one woman,
not even *the boy* [p. 220] with the brown, squinting, eyes.
I'll still be here. One can always watch.

Am I not right? You, to whom life tasted
so bitter, father, tasting mine,
that first clouded infusion of my necessities,
you kept on tasting, as I grew,
and preoccupied by the after-taste
of such a strange future, searched my misted gaze –
you, my father, who since you were dead, have often
been anxious within my innermost hopes,
and giving up calm, the kingdoms of calm
the dead own, for my bit of fate,
am I not right? And you women, am I not right,
who would love me for that small beginning
of love, for you, that I always turned away from,
because the space of your faces changed,
as I loved, into cosmic space,
where you no longer existed......When I feel
like waiting in front of the puppet theatre, no,
rather gazing at it, so intently, that at last,
to balance my gaze, an Angel must come
and take part, dragging the puppets on high.
Angel and Doll: then there's a play at last.
Then what we endlessly separate,
merely by being, comes together. Then at last

from our seasons here, the orbit
of all change emerges. Over and above us,
then, the Angel plays. See the dying
must realise that what we do here
is nothing, how full of pretext it all is,
nothing in itself. O hours of childhood,
when, behind the images, there was more
than the past, and in front of us was not the future.
We were growing, it's true, and sometimes urged that
we soon grew up, half for the sake
of those others who had nothing but their grown-up-ness.
And were, yet, on our own, happy
with Timelessness, and stood there,
in the space between world and plaything,
at a point that from first beginnings
had been marked out for pure event.

Who shows a child, just as they are? Who sets it
in its constellation, and gives the measure
of distance into its hand? Who makes a child's death
out of grey bread, that hardens, - or leaves it
inside its round mouth like the core
of a shining apple? Killers are
easy to grasp. But this: death,
the whole of death, before life,
to hold it so softly, and not live in anger,
cannot be expressed.

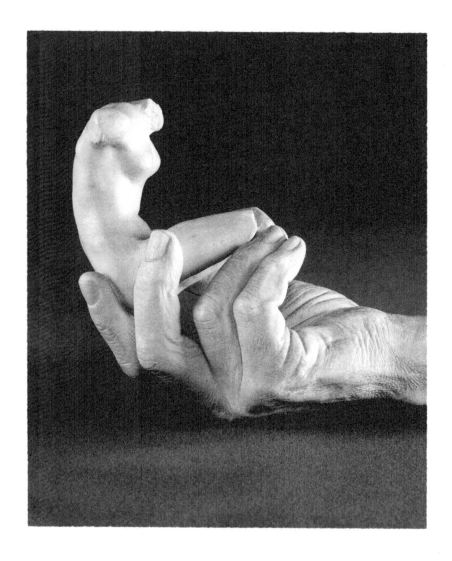

Hand of Rodin with a Female Figure, Auguste Rodin (French, 1840 – 1917)
The National Gallery of Art

THE FIFTH ELEGY

But who are they, tell me, *these Travellers* [p. 220], even more
transient than we are ourselves, urgently, from their earliest days,
wrung out for whom – to please whom,
by a never-satisfied will? Yet it wrings them,
bends them, twists them, and swings them,
throws them, and catches them again: as if from oiled
more slippery air, so they land
on the threadbare carpet, worn by their continual
leaping, this carpet
lost in the universe.
Stuck on like a plaster, as if the suburban
sky had wounded the earth there.
                              And scarcely there,
upright, there and revealed: the great
capital letter of Being.........and already the ever-returning
grasp wrings the strongest of men again, in jest,
as King August the Strong would crush
a tin plate.

Ah, and around this
centre, the rose of watching
flowers and un-flowers. Round this
stamp, this pistil, caught in the pollen
of its own flowering, fertilised
again to a shadow-fruit of disinterest,
their never-conscious, seeming-to-smile, disinterest,
gleaming lightly, on surface thinness.

There, the withered, wrinkled lifter,
an old man, only a drummer now,
shrunk in his massive hide, as though it had once
contained two men, and one was already
lying there in the churchyard, and the other had survived him,
deaf, and sometimes a little
confused in his widowed skin.

And the young one, the man, as if he were son of a neck
and a nun: taut and erectly filled
with muscle and simple-mindedness.

O you,
that a sorrow, that was still small,
once received as a plaything, in one of its
long convalescences......

You, who fall, with the thud
that only fruit knows, unripe,
a hundred times a day from the tree of mutually
built-up movement (that, swifter than water,
in a few moments, shows spring, summer and autumn),
fall, and impact on the grave:
sometimes, in half-pauses, a loving look tries
to rise from your face towards your seldom
affectionate mother: but it loses itself in your body,
whose surface consumes the shy
scarcely-attempted look.....And again
the man is clapping his hands for your leap, and before
a pain can become more distinct, close to your
constantly racing heart, a burning grows in the soles of your feet,
its source, before a few quick tears rush bodily into your eyes.
And yet, blindly,
that smile........

Standing Female Faun, Auguste Rodin (French, 1840 – 1917)
The Los Angeles County Museum of Art

Angel! O, gather it, pluck it, that small-flowered healing herb.
Make a vase, keep it safe! Place it among those joys not yet
open to us: on a lovely urn,
praise it, with flowery, swirling, inscription:

'*Subrisio Saltat: the Saltimbanque's smile*'

You, then, beloved,
you, that the loveliest delights
silently over-leapt. Perhaps
your frills are happy for you –
or the green metallic silk,
over your firm young breasts,
feels itself endlessly pampered, and needing nothing.
You, market fruit of serenity
laid out, endlessly, on all the quivering balance scales,
publicly, beneath the shoulders.

Where, oh where is the place – I carry it in my heart –
where they were still far from capable, still fell away
from each other, like coupling animals, not yet
ready for pairing: -
where the weights are still heavy:
where the plates still topple
from their vainly twirling
sticks.......

And, suddenly, in this troublesome nowhere, suddenly,
the unsayable point where the pure too-little
is changed incomprehensibly -, altered
into that empty too-much.
Where the many-placed calculation
is exactly resolved.

Squares: O square in Paris, endless show-place,

where the milliner, Madame Lamort,

winds and twists the restless trails of the earth,

endless ribbons, into new

bows, frills, flowers, rosettes, artificial fruits – all

falsely coloured, - for winter's

cheap hats of destiny.

Angel: if there were a place we know nothing of, and there,

on some unsayable carpet, lovers revealed

what here they could never master, their high daring

figures of heart's flight,

their towers of desire, their ladders,

long since standing where there was no ground, leaning,

trembling, on each other – and mastered them,

in front of the circle of watchers, the countless, soundless dead:

Would these not fling their last, ever-saved,

ever-hidden, unknown to us, eternally

valid coins of happiness in front of the finally

truly smiling pair on the silent

carpet?

THE SIXTH ELEGY

Fig-tree, for such a long time now, there has been meaning for me,
in the way you almost wholly omit to flower
and urge your pure secret, unheralded,
into the early, resolute fruit.
Like the jet of a fountain, your arched bough
drives the sap downward, then up: and it leaps from its sleep
barely waking, into the bliss of its sweetest achievement.
See: like the god into the swan

..........We, though, linger,
ah, our pride is in flowering, and, already betrayed,
we reach the late core of our final fruit.
In a few the urge to action rises so powerfully,
that they are already waiting and glowing with their heart's fullness
when the temptation to flower, like the mild night air,
touches their tender mouths, touches their eyelids:
heroes perhaps, and those chosen to vanish prematurely,
in whom Death the gardener wove different veins.
These plunge ahead: they go before their own smile,
like the team of horses in the slightly
hollowed-out relief of Karnak's victorious pharaoh.

The Age of Bronze, Auguste Rodin (French, 1840 – 1917)
The National Gallery of Art

The hero is strangely close to those who died young. Lasting
doesn't contain him. Being is his ascent: he moves on,
time and again, to enter the changed constellation
his risk entails. Few could find him there. But
Destiny, that darkly hides us, suddenly inspired,
sings him into the tempest of his onrushing world.
I hear no one like him. All at once I am pierced
by his darkened sound carried on streaming air.
Then, how gladly I would hide from the yearning: O if I,
if I were a boy, and might come to it still, and sit,
propped on the future's arms, and reading about Samson,
how his mother first bore nothing, and then all.
Was he not a hero already, O mother, in you, did not
his imperious choice begin inside you?
Thousands seethed in the womb and willed to be him,
but see: he grasped and let go, chose and achieved.
And if he shattered pillars, it was when he burst
out of the world of your flesh into the narrower world,
where he went on choosing, achieving. O mothers of heroes,
O sources of ravening rivers! Ravines into which
weeping girls have plunged
from the high heart's edge, future offerings to the son.
Because, whenever the hero stormed through the stations of love,
each heartbeat, meant for him, lifting him onward,
he turned away, stood at the end of the smiles, someone other.

THE SEVENTH ELEGY

Wooing, no longer: wooing will not be the form of your
    cry, voice that's outgrown it: true, you would cry pure as a bird,
when the season lifts him, the ascending one, almost forgetting
that he is a suffering creature, and not just a solitary heart
that it flings into brightness, to intimate heavens. Like him,
you also, would be wooing no less – so that, still invisible,
some girl would sense you, the silent one, in whom a reply
slowly wakes and grows warm, as she listens –
the glowing feeling mated to your daring feeling.
Oh and the Spring-time would comprehend – there is no place
that would not echo its voice of proclamation.
First the tiny questioning piping, that a purely affirmative day
surrounds more deeply with heightened stillness.
Then up the stairway, the stairway of calling, up to
the dreamed-of temple of future - : then the trill, fountain
that in its rising jet already anticipates falling,
in promise's play.......And the summer to come.
Not only the devotion of these unfolded forces,
not only the paths, not only the evening fields,
not only, after a late storm, the breathing freshness,
not only approaching sleep and a premonition, evenings...
also the nights! Also the high summer nights,
also the stars, the stars of this Earth!
O to be dead at last and know them eternally,
all the stars: for how, how, how to forget them!

See, I was calling my lover. But not only she
would come......Girls would come from delicate graves
and gather.....for, how could I limit
the call, once called? The buried always
still seek the Earth. – You, children, a single
thing grasped here is many times valid.
Don't think that Fate is more than a childhood across:
how often you overtook the beloved, panting,
panting after the blissful chase after nothing, into what's free.
Being here is the wonder. You knew it, girls, even you,
you who seemed dispensable, sunken – you, in the worst
streets of the cities, festering, or open
for refuse. Since an hour was given – perhaps not
so much as an hour, one that was scarcely
measurable by time's measure, between two moments, where you
had a being. Everything. Veins filled with being.
But we forget so easily what our laughing neighbour
neither acknowledges nor envies. We want to visibly
show it, while even the most visible of joys
can only display itself to us when we have changed it, from within.
Nowhere, beloved, will world be, but within. Our
life passes in change. And ever-shrinking
the outer diminishes. Where there was once a permanent house,
some conceptual structure springs up, athwart us, as fully
at home among concepts, as if it still stood in the brain.
Vast reservoirs of power are created by the spirit of the age,
formless, like the tense yearning gained from all things.
Temples are no longer known. Those extravagances
of the heart we keep, more secretly. Yes, where even one survives,
a single thing once prayed to, served, knelt before –
it stands, as it is, already there in the invisible.
Many no longer see it, but lose the chance to build it
inside themselves now, with columns, and statues, grander!

Each vague turn of the world has such disinherited ones,
to whom the former does not, and the next does not yet, belong.
Since even the next is far from mankind. Though
this should not confuse us, but strengthen in us the keeping
of still recognisable forms. This once stood among men,
stood in the midst of fate, the destroyer, stood
in the midst of not-knowing-towards-what, as if it existed, and drew
stars towards itself out of the enshrined heavens. Angel,
I'll show it to you, also, there! It will stand
in your gaze, finally upright, saved at last.
Columns, pylons, the Sphinx, the stirring thrust
of the cathedral, grey, out of a fading or alien city.

Was it not miracle? O, be astonished, Angel, since we are this,
O tell them, O great one, that we could achieve this: my breath
is too slight for this praising. So, after all, we have not
failed to make use of these spaces, these generous ones,
our spaces. (How frighteningly vast they must be,
when they are not overfull of our feelings, after thousands of years.)
But a tower was great, was it not? O Angel, it was though –
even compared to you? Chartres was great – and Music
towered still higher and went beyond us. Why even
a girl in love, oh, alone in the night, at her window,
did she not reach to your knees? –

                       Don't think that I'm wooing.
Angel, were I doing so, you would not come! Since my call
is always full of outpouring: against such a powerful
current you cannot advance. Like an outstretched
arm, my call. And its hand, opened above
for grasping, remains open, before you,
as if for defence and for warning,
wide open, Incomprehensible One.

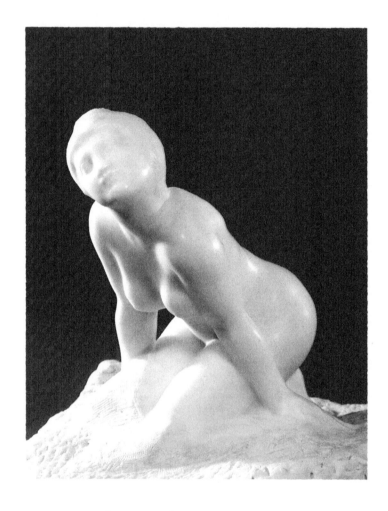

Figure of a Woman "The Sphinx", Auguste Rodin (French, 1840 – 1917)
The National Gallery of Art

THE EIGHTH ELEGY

The creature gazes into openness with all
       its eyes. But our eyes are
       as if they were reversed, and surround it,
everywhere, like barriers against its free passage.
We know what is outside us from the animal's
face alone: since we already turn
the young child round and make it look
backwards at what is settled, not that openness
that is so deep in the animal's vision. Free from death.
We alone see that: the free creature
has its progress always behind it,
and God before it, and when it moves, it moves
in eternity, as streams do.
We never have pure space in front of us,
not for a single day, such as flowers open
endlessly into. Always there is world,
and never the Nowhere without the Not: the pure,
unwatched-over, that one breathes and
endlessly knows, without craving. As a child
loses itself sometimes, one with the stillness, and
is jolted back. Or someone dies and is it.
Since near to death one no longer sees death,
and stares ahead, perhaps with the large gaze of the creature.
Lovers are close to it, in wonder, if
the other were not always there closing off the view.....
As if through an oversight it opens out
behind the other......But there is no
way past it, and it turns to world again.

Female Centaur, Auguste Rodin (French, 1840 – 1917)
The Los Angeles County Museum of Art

Always turned towards creation, we see
only a mirroring of freedom
dimmed by us. Or that an animal
mutely, calmly is looking through and through us.
This is what fate means: to be opposite,
and to be that and nothing else, opposite, forever.

If there was consciousness like ours
in the sure creature, that moves towards us
on a different track – it would drag us
round in its wake. But its own being
is boundless, unfathomable, and without a view
of its condition, pure as its outward gaze.
And where we see future it sees everything,
and itself in everything, and is healed for ever.

And yet in the warm waking creature
is the care and burden of a great sadness.
Since it too always has within it what often
overwhelms us – a memory,
as if what one is pursuing now was once
nearer, truer, and joined to us
with infinite tenderness. Here all is distance,
there it was breath. Compared to that first home
the second one seems ambiguous and uncertain.

O bliss of little creatures
that stay in the womb that carried them forever:
O joy of the midge that can still leap within,
even when it is wed: since womb is all.
And see the half-assurance of the bird,
almost aware of both from its inception,
as if it were the soul of an Etruscan,
born of a dead man in a space
with his reclining figure as the lid.
And how dismayed anything is that has to fly,
and leave the womb. As if it were
terrified of itself, zig-zagging through the air, as a crack
runs through a cup. As the track
of a bat rends the porcelain of evening.

And we: onlookers, always, everywhere,
always looking into, never out of, everything.
It fills us. We arrange it. It collapses.
We arrange it again, and collapse ourselves.

Who has turned us round like this, so that,
whatever we do, we always have the aspect
of one who leaves? Just as they
will turn, stop, linger, for one last time,
on the last hill, that shows them all their valley - ,
so we live, and are always taking leave.

THE NINTH ELEGY

Why, if it could begin as laurel, and be spent so,
this space of Being, a little darker than all
the surrounding green, with little waves at the edge
of every leaf (like a breeze's smile) - : why then
have to be human – and shunning destiny
long for destiny?....
                        Oh, not because happiness exists,
that over-hasty profit from imminent loss,
not out of curiosity, or to practice the heart,
which could exist in the laurel......
But because being here is much, and because all
that's here seems to need us, the ephemeral, that
strangely concerns us. We: the most ephemeral. Once,
for each thing, only once. Once, and no more. And we too,
once. Never again. But this
once, to have been, though only once,
to have been an earthly thing – seems irrevocable.

And so we keep pushing on, and trying to achieve it,
trying to contain it in our simple hands,
in the overflowing gaze and the speechless heart.
Trying to become it. Whom to give it to? We would
hold on to it for ever....Ah, what, alas, do we
take into that other dimension? Not the gazing which we
slowly learned here, and nothing that happened. Nothing.
Suffering then. Above all, then, the difficulty,
the long experience of love, then – what is
wholly unsayable. But later,
among the stars, what use is it: it is better unsayable.
Since the traveller does not bring a handful of earth
from mountain-slope to valley, unsayable to others, but only
a word that was won, pure, a yellow and blue
gentian. Are we here, perhaps, for saying: house,
bridge, fountain, gate, jug, fruit-tree, window –
at most: column, tower......but for saying, realise,
oh, for a saying such as the things themselves would never
have profoundly said. Is not the secret intent
of this discreet Earth to draw lovers on,
so that each and every thing is delight within their feeling?
Threshold: what is it for two
lovers to be wearing their own threshold of the ancient door
a little, they too, after the many before them,
and before those to come......., simple.

Memorial Relief (Hand of a Child), Auguste Rodin (French, 1840 – 1917)
The National Gallery of Art

Here is the age of the sayable: here is its home.
Speak, and be witness. More than ever
the things of experience are falling away, since
what ousts and replaces them is an act with no image.
An act, under a crust that will split, as soon as
the business within outgrows it, and limit itself differently.
Between the hammers, our heart
lives on, as the tongue
between the teeth, that
in spite of them, keeps praising.

Praise the world to the Angel, not the unsayable: you
can't impress him with glories of feeling: in the universe,
where he feels more deeply, you are a novice. So show
him a simple thing, fashioned in age after age,
that lives close to hand and in sight.
Tell him things. He'll be more amazed: as you were,
beside the rope-maker in Rome, or the potter beside the Nile.
Show him how happy things can be, how guiltless and ours,
how even the cry of grief decides on pure form,
serves as a thing, or dies into a thing: transient,
they look to us for deliverance, we, the most transient of all.
Will us to change them completely, in our invisible hearts,
into – oh, endlessly, into us! Whoever, in the end, we are.

Earth, is it not this that you want: to rise

invisibly in us? – Is that not your dream,

to be invisible, one day? – Earth! Invisible!

What is your urgent command if not transformation?

Earth, beloved, I will. O, believe me, you need

no more Spring-times to win me: only one,

ah, one, is already more than my blood can stand.

Namelessly, I have been truly yours, from the first.

You were always right, and your most sacred inspiration

is that familiar Death.

See I live. On what? Neither childhood nor future

grows less......Excess of being

wells up in my heart.

THE TENTH ELEGY

S ome day, in the emergence from this fierce insight,
  let me sing jubilation and praise to assenting Angels.
  Let not a single one of the cleanly-struck hammers of my heart
deny me, through a slack, or a doubtful, or
a broken string. Let my streaming face
make me more radiant: let my secret weeping
bear flower. O, how dear you will be to me, then, Nights
of anguish. Inconsolable sisters, why did I not
kneel more to greet you, lose myself more
in your loosened hair? We, squanderers of pain.
How we gaze beyond them into duration's sadness,
to see if they have an end. Though they are nothing but
our winter-suffering foliage, our dark evergreen,
one of the seasons of our inner year – not only
season - : but place, settlement, camp, soil, dwelling.

Strange, though, alas, the streets of Grief-City,
where, in the artificiality of a drowned-out false
stillness, the statue cast from the mould of emptiness bravely
swaggers: the gilded noise, the flawed memorial.
O, how an Angel would utterly trample their market of solace,
bounded by the Church, bought ready for use:
untouched, disenchanted and shut like the post-office on Sunday.
Beyond though, the outskirts are always alive with the fair.
Swings of freedom! Divers and jugglers of zeal!
And the figures at the shooting range of easy luck,
targets that shake tinnily whenever some better marksman
hits one. From applause at his luck

he staggers on further: as booths for every taste
are wooing him, drumming, and bawling. Here's something
special, only for adults, to view: how money is got, anatomy,
not just to amuse: the private parts of money,
all of it, the whole thing, the act, - to instruct and make
potent.......O, but just beyond
behind the last hoarding, plastered with adverts for 'Deathless',
that bitter beer that tastes sweet to its drinkers,
as long as they chew fresh distractions along with it......
just at the back of the hoardings, just behind them, it's real.
Children are playing, lovers are holding each other – to the side,
sombrely, in the sparse grass, and dogs are following their nature.
The youth is drawn on, further: perhaps it's a young
Lament he loves......He comes to the field, beyond her. She says:
'It's far. We live out there....'

               'Where?' And the youth follows.
He is moved by her manner. Her shoulders, her neck – perhaps
she's from a notable family. But he leaves her, turns round,
looks back, waves.......What's the point? She's a Lament.

Only those who died young, in their first state
of timeless equanimity, that of being weaned,
follow her lovingly. She waits
for girls and befriends them. She shows them gently
what she is wearing. Pearls of grief and the fine
veils of suffering. – With youths she walks on
in silence.

La Douleur (de La Porte), Auguste Rodin (French, 1840 – 1917)
The Los Angeles County Museum of Art

But there, where they live, in the valley, one of the older Laments,
takes to the youth, when he questions: - 'We were,'
she says, 'a large family once, we Laments. Our ancestors
worked the mines on that mountain-range: among men
you'll sometimes find a lump of polished primal grief,
or the lava of frozen rage from some old volcano.
Yes, that came from there. We used to be rich.' -

And she leads him gently through the wide landscape of Lament,
shows him the columns of temples, the ruins
of castles, from which the lords of Lament
ruled the land, wisely. Shows him the tall
Tear-trees, and the fields of flowering Sadness,
(The living know it as only a tender shrub.)
shows him the herds of Grief, grazing – and sometimes
a startled bird, flying low through their upward glance,
will inscribe on the far distance the written form of its lonely cry –
At evening she leads him to the graves of the elders
of the race of Laments, the sibyls and prophets.
But as night falls, so they move more softly, and soon,
like a moon, the all-guarding
sepulchre rises. Brother to that of the Nile,
the tall Sphinx, the secret chamber's
countenance.
And they are astonished by the regal head, that forever,
silently, positioned the human face
in the scale of the stars.

His sight cannot grasp it, still dizzied
by early death. But her gaze
frightens an owl from behind the rim of the crown,
and the bird brushes, with slow skimming flight, along the cheek,
the one with the richer curve,
and inscribes the indescribable
outline, on the new
hearing born out of death, as though
on the doubly-unfolded page of a book.

And higher: the stars. New stars, of Grief-Land.
Slowly the Lament names them: 'There,
see: the *Rider*, the *Staff*, and that larger constellation
they name *Fruit-Garland*. Then, further, towards the Pole:
the *Cradle*, the *Way*, the *Burning Book*, the *Doll*, the *Window*.
But in the southern sky, pure as on
the palm of a sacred hand, the clearly shining *M*,
that stands for the Mothers......'

But the dead must go on, and in silence the elder Lament
leads him as far as the ravine,
where the fountain of joy
glistens in moonlight. With awe
she names it saying: 'Among men
this is a load-bearing river.'

They stand at the foot of the mountains.
And there she embraces him, weeping.

He climbs alone, on the mountains of primal grief.
And not once do his footsteps sound from his silent fate.

But if the endlessly dead woke a symbol in us,
see, they would point perhaps to the catkins,
hanging from bare hazels, or
they would intend the rain, falling on dark soil in Spring-time. –

And we, who think of ascending
joy, would feel the emotion,
that almost dismays us,
when a joyful thing falls.

THE FOUNTAIN OF JOY

A NEW COMMENTARY ON RILKE'S DUINO ELEGIES

Eternal Spring, Auguste Rodin (French, 1840 – 1917)
The Los Angeles County Museum of Art

INTRODUCTION

An Elegy is a song of lamentation, often written in an elegiac metre, especially a lament for the dead, though the term is often vaguely used of other poetry. Rilke began his Duino Elegies at Schloss Duino near Trieste (on a rocky Adriatic headland, north-west of the city) where he stayed as a guest in the winter of 1911/12, and completed them in early February 1922 at the Chateau de Muzot (*pronounced Muzotte*) near Sierre in Switzerland (south of Berne, and east of Montreux). His Sonnets to Orpheus were completed contemporaneously, as a complementary work, a song of praise, enhancing the song of lament of the Elegies, which nevertheless despite their lamentation represent reconciliation with life, and seek to bear witness to its underlying fountain of joy, the source and spring from which the stream of acceptance and creativity flows that allows us to endure our transient and often painful existence. Lament and joy for Rilke are two sides of the same coin of being, and his main concern is to reveal them in his poetry as aspects of the single whole, the double-realm.

One must be wary of Rilke's own comments (and those of others) about his poetry. His tendency to hyperbole in his letters, and the continuous creation and cultivation of his image as the inspired poet, prove honey-tongued in a seductive, and compelling way. His style is a hypnotic one, and in some respects antipathetic to our own age (it can seem sickly and specious in its claims, those of his commentators sycophantic and excessive), yet the style should not be allowed to obscure the enormous power, and strange beauty of the Elegies. While many of his letters concerning them merely express his great and convoluted relief at having completed them, he also offered a few incisive comments, in particular writing to his Polish translator Witold Hulewicz in November 1925 '*We of the present are never satisfied by the world of time...transience everywhere plunges into the depths of being...it is our task to print this temporal, perishable earth so painfully, passionately and deeply into ourselves, that its essence is resurrected again, invisibly, within us...the Elegies show this, the work of endlessly converting the visible, tangible world we love into the invisible vibrations and tremors of our own nature...*' This is Rilke's concept of the temple within. And it is his adherence to the interior life, and the re-creation and transformation of the exterior world within the mind, that gives his poetry its distinctive other-worldly feel, its sometimes ghostly even deathly countenance, its resonance derived as much from the non-existent and no-longer-living as from the visible and human. That adherence creates a style which runs the risks of affectation, and over-aestheticism at the superficial level, of world-rejection and morbidity at the deepest level. Both are threats to the tightrope-walker that Rilke represents as a poet. Because they are constant threats to all artists working in this age of modernity (there is no such thing yet as post-modernity), Rilke's example is still vital and cogent for us. In many respects it is Rilke who is Baudelaire's heir, though a very different poet. He completes an interior journey that Baudelaire commenced: he is a post-Romantic who is the heir of Romanticism, of the turning inward and away from the social as a means of modern salvation. Religion is subsumed by naked spirituality, and some of the trappings of religion become a means of expression for that spirituality without necessarily indicating conventional beliefs. With Rilke, concept is always more important than external reality, and the idea which generates feeling and disturbs our depths more important than faith in some outward manifestation of it. Mind is more important for Rilke than the world, symbolic being than actual being, though he would have protested that on the contrary he was a world-lover not a world-rejecter.

His conceptualisation, complicated by poetic personification and empathetic fallacy, is a major risk to his message, since it may undermine the ideas being expressed by confusing the audience. Are Rilke's Angels, for example, real or imaginary? To Rilke, I genuinely believe, it did not matter. What the concept of the Angel represented to him, and its effect on our human condition and aspirations, were and are much more important. Unfortunately, readers may seek an objective correlative for Rilke's angels, and be disappointed or deluded. Religion is not his aim. Spirituality and reconciliation with life are. Because he was so threatened by modernity, by the real and philosophical fragility of our existence, and the nausea and terror which that fragile existence can generate, he sought through mind and poetry a view of life which might offset the pain. The Elegies are that view. While the resolution, in praise, of the Sonnets to Orpheus might not always convince, the Elegies which are the diagnosis of our condition frequently ring true, and in a deep way that can change one's own view of being. It is a view that he expressed in his beautiful-constructed poem, The

Dove, and in a letter of 1923: '*Whoever does not sometimes give full consent, and a joyous consent, to the dreadfulness of life, can never possess the unutterable richness and power of existence, can only walk at its edge, and one day, when judgement is given, will have been neither living nor dead. To show this identity of terror and bliss, these two faces of the same immortal head, indeed this single face...this is the true significance and purpose of the Elegies and the Sonnets to Orpheus.*' Rilke here echoes Dante's positioning of the spiritually neutral at the Gates of Hell, in Inferno Canto III, those '*who have lost the good of the intellect*' and: '*lived without praise and without blame*'. He believed the true life to demand more from us than spiritual passivity in the face of the joyful and the terrible.

Rilke often expresses the feeling that his works were given to him and came from outside himself. Clearly, this is a common feeling among creative people that stems from the activities of the sub-conscious or supra-conscious mind, feeding on elements from the world around it. Concepts and symbols, ideas and things carry with them a vast weight of social and personal significance, and that weight is greater than the individual and yet within the individual. So that the mind's being in the world and the world's being in the mind are complementary, indissoluble aspects of thought and feeling. It is just such 'artistic' and seductively spiritual feelings as Rilke's of the works being 'given' that we must be wary of when reading him, lest he be diminished by the aura of some milieu of preciousness. As often with Rilke the feeling is valid and important, but the language may seem to slide away from modernity back into religiosity or a kind of anticipatory new-ageism. Yet the underlying vision in the Elegies is hard and penetrating. The words of the letters and some of the poems where his intensity was relaxed somewhat can seem artificial and shallow. He is never slight or uninteresting, but he can be his own worst enemy in stylistic self-indulgence.

Rilke is always self-centred, but always has wider relevance, is always personal but has claims to wider universality. He saw his constant task as transformation, of himself into another, of the world into the mind, of external phenomena into internal, things into thoughts, being into consciousness and becoming. That task can sometimes seem wearying in its lack of spontaneity. That seductive voice can seem the voice of the tempter, proclaiming as fact what is only surmise, and as truth what is only poetry. He specialised in a kind of strangeness, because he required it '*as expressive of something within*'. Poetry is a struggle with language, and the proof or otherwise of Rilke's success in that struggle lies in his works. The critical faculty, the refusal to grant acquiescence without reflection, is an essential quality in reading Rilke and the Elegies. The writing is often beautiful, but it is right to ask also, is it true? Sometimes he can seem to have reached the '*deeper dimensions of the inner being*' he tried for. Sometimes he can seem to merely reflect a futility, a sterility of Western civilisation, affected by a world war, and decades of prior over-refinement. An antidote to too much reading, and too much Rilke, is to go out into nature, or talk and laugh with another human being. Nevertheless this hyper-conscious, subtle and semi-solipsistic work can reach out to us, when we are least expecting it, and persuade again, in its hypnotic tones, that the world of Ideas is not a lie, and that Symbols and Language can lead beyond event and temporality to a place from whose perspective all time is eternal, and all space seems internal. He was willing to face up to the immense pain and suffering within life, and to the knowledge of its swift passing, and his art he saw as giving '*now and then, a perhaps clearer meaning to endurance.*'

THE FIRST ELEGY

Who, if I cried out, would hear me among the Angelic
Orders? And even if one were to suddenly
take me to its heart, I would vanish into its
stronger existence. For beauty is nothing but
the beginning of terror, that we are still able to bear,
and we revere it so, because it calmly disdains
to destroy us. Every Angel is terror.

Rilke begins with an intense questioning cry. Yet still an ambiguous cry. Who among the Angels would hear so small and insignificant an entity as himself crying out, since the Angels both exist and comprehend all being, encompassing it inwardly? Is that what he means? Or: who or what is there to respond to *him* if *he* cried out, as something seemingly responded to the devout who cried out in previous ages, a Saint Theresa for example? Is the Angel a real existent capable of responding, or a concept indicating *'the world no longer from the human point of view, but as it is within the angel'* (Letter, 1915) a perspective or act of transformation which he saw as his real task. *'The Angel of the Elegies has nothing to do with the angel of the Christian heaven,* he wrote, *'...the Angel of the Elegies is that creature in whom the transformation of the visible into the invisible, which we perform, appears already complete.'* (Letter, 1925) The Angel seems to represent to Rilke an Idea of perfect internality, beyond human contradictions and limitations, *'that being who attests to the recognition of a higher level of reality in the invisible – Terrifying, therefore, to us because we, its lovers and transformers, still cling to the visible'*. The external existence of such a consciousness is irrelevant to Rilke, since the idea of it, which is its spiritual existence, is within us as concept. *'Here is the angel, who doesn't exist, and the devil who doesn't exist, and the human being who does exist stands between them, and (I can't help saying it) their unreality makes him more real to me.'* (Letter, 1922) For the Angel, Rilke explained in 1925, all the buildings (for example) consumed by the past exist because they have become invisible, while whatever still stands is already invisible within the angel, that agent of transformation, of complete eternal consciousness. But, lest these angels be confused with the Christian angels, his own spiritual experience was increasingly remote from Christianity, as he says in a letter of 1923 *'The Christian experience enters less and less into consideration'*, and in 1925 *'not though, in the Christian sense (from which I more and more passionately withdraw)'*

The Angel is a conceit, a symbol of the non-existent superhuman consciousness. Whether Rilke had a belief in the Angel's external reality is hard to say, but some of the more dubious areas into which he strays are ultimately of less interest than the idea of internalising the universe within consciousness with which he is primarily occupied. He is certainly not utilising the concepts of organised and traditional religion. For example, he said: *'By making the mistake of applying Catholic conceptions…to the Elegies or Sonnets, one is withdrawing completely from their point of departure, and preparing for oneself a more and more fundamental misunderstanding'* (Letter, 1925).

In the first few lines of the opening Elegy, above, Rilke indicates the all-encompassing power of completed transformation, its *stronger existence*, and the terror it represents to us, the terror of eternity for finite beings, of a perspective beyond society for the social animal, and of a view of existence which stands on time rather than being of time. In that terror Rilke finds a strange beauty, and then generalises that beauty itself is full of incipient terror because it draws us, without destroying us, into the orbit of that deeper perception where we see the transience, our limitations, our incapacity for transformation, and a depth and complexity beyond our grasp. His generalisation is only partially valid. Beauty may equally be an indication of form with no designs on us, delight with no authority over us, and relationship without possession. Rilke has set a hidden goal here of movement towards the Angel, a goal perhaps of Western and Middle Eastern Civilisation but not necessarily that of the East. The Taoist way of life for example would suggest that rather than transformation of nature we can seek identification with nature, rather than goals we can seek spontaneity, rather than projecting ourselves onto the world we can accept its flow of energies with humility. Here, in the Elegies, the Idea is also an Ideal, a complete consciousness in which life and death are absorbed, transformed and realised within. Is Rilke also revealing his own failures of relationship, his own desire for an escape from those failures, into a relationship where the Other is simply transformed into the Self, and is therefore a pure narcissism? Yet he at the same time recognises the impossibility (the undesirability?) for a human being, and not an Angel, of such aspirations.

And so I hold myself back and swallow the cry
of a darkened sobbing. Ah, who then can
we make use of? Not Angels: not men,

He steps back from the attempt, recognising its futility, but lamenting the impossibility of achieving the Angel's state of consciousness. Who then, he asks, can we make use of in our task of transformation, who can we turn to in our need for consolation and help? Neither Angels, nor, says Rilke, human beings. 'For when, on *my return from a thorough immersion in things and animals,*' after composing his New Poems, '*I was looking forward to a course in humanity, lo and behold, the next realm, that of angels was set before me: thus I have by-passed people and am now looking back cordially at them.*' (Letter, 1913). Rilke seems to evade the human relationship, claiming that human beings cannot assist with the task of transformation. Why: presumably because we are betwixt and between, self-conscious and aware and capable of transformation, but incapable of performing it for another?

and the resourceful creatures see clearly
that we are not really at home
in the interpreted world.

The resourceful and enduring creatures of the natural world, Rilke suggest, detect our uneasiness with the world of language and thought which we have created internally, our interpreted world. They are a part of nature without complex language-driven thought and therefore transformation, and so unable to console us or help because they lie on the pre-conscious side of reality, with things. The contemporary assertion of a continuum of self-awareness and empathy extending through the animal realm and including the human species is clearly not envisioned or is significantly under-developed here. Rilke nevertheless expressed his own empathy with creatures in the New Poems, even while treating them generally as passive vessels driven by sensation and non-introspective thought and feeling. The eighth Elegy will develop his ideas regarding the creature-world further.

> *Perhaps there remains*
> *some tree on a slope, that we can see*
> *again each day: there remains to us yesterday's street,*
> *and the thinned-out loyalty of a habit*
> *that liked us, and so stayed, and never departed.*

Perhaps consolation remains in things, incapable of transformation and therefore soothing in their neutrality, in familiar places, and in the seeming loyalty of long-lasting habit and routine. Rilke's frequent anthropomorphism is evident here in his personification of 'habit'.

> *Oh, and the night, the night, when the wind full of space*
> *wears out our faces – whom would she not stay for,*
> *the longed-for, gentle, disappointing one, whom the solitary heart*
> *with difficulty stands before.*

Night is the vast silent window onto the universe, from which a flow of energy comes that passes over our upturned faces. Here Night is given a female aspect. Intention-less and indifferent to humanity, the darkness remains, accessible to everyone. She is desired as a time and place of solace, gentle in her veiled aspects, disappointing in that she is careless of the individual and neutral in her favours, being ultimately purposeless and unable to satisfy our longings. The solitary heart stands before her with difficulty since to face the universe is to face oneself, the hardest task of all.

Is she less heavy for lovers?
Ah, they only hide their fate between themselves.
Do you not know yet?

Rilke asks himself (the ambiguous *you* in the Elegies may mean the reader or, rhetorically, the poet himself, frequently both) whether the darkness and indifference of the universe, which makes no response to our cries, is alleviated by love for another human being? His answer is that love conceals the universe because lovers are turned towards each other hiding the great darkness. The weight of being therefore becomes a temporary lightness, and fate is veiled by human intensity.

Throw the emptiness out of your arms
to add to the spaces we breathe; maybe the birds
will feel the expansion of air, in more intimate flight.

The poet urges himself to hurl the emptiness that represents the absence of another loved human being into the air, so as to add to the breathable space, and perhaps cause the birds to fly with more fervour and passion.

Yes, the Spring-times needed you deeply. Many a star
must have been there for you so you might feel it. A wave
lifted towards you out of the past, or, as you walked
past an open window, a violin
gave of itself. All this was their mission.
But could you handle it?

Other aspects of the world also remain and give consolation. Rilke suggests that in a sense they 'need' our presence, in order to become subjects for transformation and be taken into the inner universe of consciousness. Springtime and star in that sense 'wait' for us to recognise them. Similarly a wave lifts towards us in memory, or is itself a wave of memory, prompting our recognition. And the sound of a violin, almost independent of human agency, itself waves of pressure in air, takes on the aspect of a thing. Rilke elsewhere (*Der Nachbar*) identified the sound with the lonely wind-filled night, playing on a hundred instruments the music of consolation. He asks himself, and us, whether we are capable of taking on the task of transformation, whether we are vast enough to take these things inwards and transform them into consciousness, the hidden interior universe, and so fulfil their mission.

Here, the reader must accept both the personification of things, and their being endowed with a kind of intent. It is again an example of his style, a mode of speech, which asserts a position that the poet may not rationally hold. Was he an animist? I doubt it. The poetic expression highlights the passive yet, to the mind, seemingly expectant aspect of the outside world in certain moods. But is that sufficient evidence to conclude that Rilke believed in the neutral universe possessing intention?

Were you not always,
still, distracted by expectation, as if all you experienced,
like a Beloved, came near to you? (Where could you contain her,
with all the vast strange thoughts in you
going in and out, and often staying the night.)

Again addressing himself, the poet identifies his own longing and failed expectation of some deep response from the universe, a response which would be akin to the approach of a beloved person, and also his failed expectation of human love. '*I could be contented with everything, if only it were entirely mine again, and did not keep discharging itself into longing.*' (Letter, 1913).... '*and yet why, since my destiny is, as it were, to pass by the human, to reach the uttermost.*' (Letter, early 1913) He reminds himself here again of his inadequacy for human relationship, given the degree to which he is occupied by vast strange thoughts to the exclusion of other modes of being.

But if you are yearning, then sing the lovers: for long
their notorious feelings have not been immortal enough.
Those, you almost envied them, the forsaken, that you
found as loving as those who were satisfied.

If the poet must yearn, then longing might lead him to the celebration of famous lovers, and thereby to carry out an interior transformation, an immortalisation of such feelings. But Rilke turns not to fulfilled relationship for his exemplars, but to unrequited lovers, those whose love was one-sided. Since the universe does not respond to our love for it, such lonely lovers more accurately exemplify our existential longing. Rilke in 1912 said: '*I have no window on human beings, that is certain....they have been communicating with me almost entirely through two examples....those who have died young and, still more unconditionally, purely, inexhaustibly: the woman who loves.*' He then quotes as examples of unrequited love, Gaspara Stampa, Louise Labé, certain Venetian courtesans, and, 'above all', the nun Marianna Alcoforada, and comments how '*on the side of the woman, everything performed, endured and accomplished contrasts with man's absolute insufficiency in love.*' Rilke holds up as example both the extreme self-denial of such love and its one-sided nature, indicating again his own difficulty with reciprocal relationship. He argues that such love is heroic and infinite. (It is equally valid however to consider it extreme, if not perverse, and so our own love for the universe might seem perverse and extreme. Why then does it not, while such unrequited love for an object capable of responding may? Precisely because the universe is not capable of responding, and therefore our love for it is a gift, just as its beauty and complexity seems a gift to us.) His argument is an example of how Rilke seduces, but may also distort. He takes an example from one sphere of our behaviour and feeling and applies it to another. The parallel seems seductive, but the argument may be invalid. Readers must decide for themselves.

Note here also his view of the function of song. Singing is praising, and the theme of praise overt in the Sonnets to Orpheus, here secondary and muted, is vital to the Elegies also. The poet is here to praise, see for example the poem Praise, and Sonnets to Orpheus I:7. Praising is a means of transformation, of taking the world inwards and also expressing it in timeless art.

Begin,

always as new, the unattainable praising:

think: the hero prolongs himself, even his falling

was only a pretext for being, his latest rebirth.

But lovers are taken back by exhausted Nature

into herself, as if there were not the power

to make them again.

The Hero is another example of a human role in contact with a wider fate, and a possible exemplar, but the hero is already re-incarnated through time and human memory, and perpetuated in art. His (her?) arc of being, even his death itself, is his reason for being, and therefore a perpetual shining symbol or mask (think of Achilles), behind which the human can stand. The lovers however are forgotten, undifferentiated, victims of love. The hero's fate is somehow chosen and intentional, the unrequited lover's an unintended and unfortunate consequence of their love. While the masks of Achilles and Hector identify them, and may be resurrected endlessly, the mask of Love hides an anonymous face, and yet each love is unique. It is easy however to think of counter-examples to this distinction, and it is perhaps rather unconvincing. More significant, however is Rilke's singling out of the unrequited lovers and the hero for further poetic treatment.

Have you remembered

Gastara Stampa [p. 220] *sufficiently yet, that any girl,*

whose lover has gone, might feel from that

intenser example of love: 'Could I only become like her?'

Should not these ancient sufferings be finally

fruitful for us? Isn't it time that, loving,

we freed ourselves from the beloved, and, trembling, endured

as the arrow endures the bow, so as to be, in its flight,

something more than itself? For staying is nowhere.

Gaspara Stampa, the sixteenth-century lover and poetess, is an example. Rilke argues here for a like acceptance of solitude, and one-sided love. He asserts that a more intense, perhaps purer love can exist when that love is not returned, and equally not fulfilled, as it apparently was for say Saint Theresa, in religious devotion. It is human love, within the non-religious realm he is talking about, and in Requiem he preaches even within human love the need to practice letting go, since holding on comes easily. He asserted in a Letter that *'in the end no one in life can help anyone else in life…one is alone. All companionship can comprise only the strengthening of two neighbouring solitudes, whereas all one calls giving oneself is harmful in nature to companionship.'* There is a significant degree of truth in this, but Rilke's extreme interpretation of relationship and love, perhaps even his incapacity for it, must be born in mind when reading the Elegies.

> *Voices, voices. Hear then, my heart, as only*
> *saints have heard: so that the mighty call*
> *raised them from the earth: they, though, knelt on*
> *impossibly and paid no attention:*
> *such was their listening. Not that you could withstand*
> *God's voice: far from it. But listen to the breath,*
> *the unbroken message that creates itself from the silence.*

Rilke is invoking the voices of his exemplars, those who moved towards infinity and extremity, those who point us towards the edge of life, and he compares the poet's listening with the saints' rapture, though he is quick to downplay the comparison. The poet would be equally incapable of withstanding the clasp of the angel or the voice of the deity. The voice he is listening for is that of the unbroken message from the silent realm of the dead, unbroken because repeated in all generations – and regarding that repetition he once wrote of those who, with regard to failed love and sexuality, *'lose it only for themselves, and still hand it on, like a sealed letter, without knowing it'*.

It rushes towards you now, from those youthfully dead.
Whenever you entered, didn't their fate speak to you,
quietly, in churches in Naples or Rome?
Or else an inscription exaltedly impressed itself on you,
as lately the tablet in Santa Maria Formosa [p. 220].
What do they will of me? That I should gently remove
the semblance of injustice, that slightly, at times,
hinders their spirits from a pure moving-on.

Rilke hears the voices of those who died young, *'In Padua…in Bologna, in Venice, in Rome, everywhere, I stood as a pupil of death: stood before death's boundless knowledge and let myself be educated. You must remember too how in the churches of Genoa and Verona, those youthful forms rest, without envy for our coming and going, fulfilled internally, as if in their death-spasms they had bitten into the fruit of life for the first time, and were now, forever, savouring its unfathomable sweetness'* (Letter, 1914). Whether or not one takes exception to this poetic conceit of the dead still possessing a kind of consciousness, and achieving a fulfilment, which may seem particularly perverse on Rilke's part if one is not religious, the poetic point is to lead Rilke into a passage concerning the realm of death, which he seeks to integrate in all his poetry into the realm of life, seeing both as a whole, a double-realm, within consciousness, where reality is transformed. It is not clear whether Rilke believed in an objective correlative to the realm of death, other than as an echoing absence, but he wishes to make room within the universe of consciousness for death, which otherwise would be un-transformed and lie outside consciousness. The reader must decide whether that is impossible for human beings or not and whether consciousness is or is not inevitably bounded by conception and death. Either way it leaves the possibility open for consciousness to work on states of life and death as content for its reflections, and Rilke's primary concern is for wholeness, for praise and lamentation to come together in celebration, in this life. *'Only from the side of death (when death is not accepted as an extinction but imagined as an altogether surpassing intensity), I believe, is it possible to do justice to love'.* Note the word *imagined.* (Letter, 1920) His argument is that *'every one of our deepest raptures makes itself independent of duration and passage; indeed they stand vertically on the courses of life, just as death, too, stands vertically on them; they have more in common with death than with all our vital aims and movements.'* Rilke takes the risk of associating with the deathly, in order to bring it into the whole. And because he believes he sees that whole, he needs to work to remove the sense of injustice we feel when contemplating the early dead. It is helpful to visualise this as a process taking place within the collective human consciousness, a means of releasing us all from the thrall of death and seeing death as a process within the species. Rilke sets himself a daunting but, he believed, essential goal: *'we, in the meaning of the Elegies, are these transformers of the earth, our whole existence, the flights and plunges of our love, all fit us for this task'*. (Letter 1925) And by transformation he means *'the transformation of the visible into the invisible'*, which is *'a higher degree of reality'*. He now goes on to investigate the second realm.

> *It is truly strange to no longer inhabit the earth,*
> *to no longer practice customs barely acquired,*
> *not to give a meaning of human futurity*
> *to roses, and other expressly promising things:*
> *no longer to be what one was in endlessly anxious hands,*
> *and to set aside even one's own*
> *proper name like a broken plaything.*
> *Strange: not to go on wishing one's wishes. Strange*
> *to see all that was once in place, floating*
> *so loosely in space. And it's hard being dead,*
> *and full of retrieval, before one gradually feels*
> *a little eternity.*

Rilke here tries to characterise and describe the state of being newly dead, as though it were a state of mind, of strangeness. The dead are unable to practise the life of the living, are no longer part of the world's cycle of creation and growth, no longer have identity or purpose or desires. They are in some strange state of consciousness which depends on processing the contents of memory, in order that they might transform themselves into a part of the timeless region.

Though the living
all make the error of drawing too sharp a distinction.
Angels (they say) would often not know whether
they moved among living or dead. The eternal current
sweeps all the ages, within it, through both the spheres,
forever, and resounds above them in both.

But, Rilke claims, this is a human error of perspective, because to the Angel, that concept of the completed consciousness, in which all has been processed and transformed into the invisible, there is no sharp distinction between life and death. Both are part of the whole, the eternal current or flow, in which everything is now contemporaneous (rather like Dante's afterlife where representatives of all the past ages co-exist), and which comprises both spheres of reality, the living and the dead, and resonates within them.

Finally they have no more need of us, the early-departed,
weaned gently from earthly things, as one outgrows
the mother's mild breast. But we, needing
such great secrets, for whom sadness is often
the source of a blessed progress, could we exist without them?

There is no need therefore to feel sorry for the early dead, they are weaned away from our life, and part of a greater whole. It is rather we who have need of them, as representatives from whom we can learn the double realm, and the wholeness of being, transforming it in consciousness, much as we need and feel contemporaneous with the minds of past ages, in our multi-faceted experience of reality.

Is it a meaningless story how once, in the grieving for Linos [p. 220],
first music ventured to penetrate arid rigidity,
so that, in startled space, which an almost godlike youth
suddenly left forever, the emptiness first felt
the quivering that now enraptures us, and comforts, and helps.

Rilke finally ends this first Elegy by referring back to the myth of Linos, a youth, the greatest of early musicians, child of one of the Muses, in one variant of the myth a brother of Orpheus, killed by the god of music and the arts, Apollo, in a fit of jealousy. His death was remembered at Delphi with chanted dirges, the *linoi*, and the laments spread throughout Greece and even, according to Pausanias, to Egypt in the form of the dirges to Maneros, the Egyptian spirit of the harvest. The myth suggests an ancient vegetation ritual, with later accretions. Rilke associates the death of Linos, in a further variant, with the invention of music itself, so that the emptiness of death became an empty space now filled with vibration, and death itself a second realm, resonating in harmony with the primary realm of the living. He wrote: '*Death is the side of life turned away from us, un-illuminated by us: we must try to achieve the greatest possible consciousness of our existence, which is at home in both of these unlimited provinces, and inexhaustibly nourished by both…there is neither a here nor a beyond, but only the great unity, in which the Angels those beings that surpass us, are at home.*' (Letter, 1925)

To summarise, Rilke has introduced us, in the first Elegy, to the Angel, imagined as the perfect transformer of visible existence into the invisible. Human beings are much more limited and incapable of such complete insight and transformation, occupied as we are with our habitual lives, though troubled by longing. But we may find indications of our primary task in the existence and fate of unrequited lovers, heroes, and the early-dead, who point beyond our constrained life of habit towards infinity. It is possible we might free ourselves from our habitual pre-occupations and learn a new way of integrating both life and death, to give a clearer vision of the whole of being, which comprises both realms. Rilke's next step will be to consider visible human life in more detail, as if he were Orpheus descending into the shades.

THE SECOND ELEGY

Every Angel is terror. And yet,
ah, knowing you, I invoke you, almost deadly
birds of the soul. Where are the days of Tobias [p. 220],
when one of the most radiant of you stood at the simple threshold,
disguised somewhat for the journey and already no longer awesome
(Like a youth, to the youth looking out curiously).
Let the Archangel [p. 220] *now, the dangerous one, from behind the stars,*
take a single step down and toward us: our own heart,
beating on high would beat us down. What are you?

Rilke again posits the concept of the Angels, the birds of the soul, first invoking the angel Raphael, the healer, who cures blindness, here spiritual blindness, though Tobit's actual blindness in the Book of Tobit. And then the dangerous Archangel, from behind the stars, who in Christian mythology would be Michael, the commander of the army of God and therefore dangerous, the only one named as an Archangel in the canonical Biblical texts. Greater than we humans, what are the angels, Rilke asks, and proceeds to answer.

Early successes, Creation's favourite ones,
mountain-chains, ridges reddened by dawns
of all origin — pollen of flowering godhead,
junctions of light, corridors, stairs, thrones,
spaces of being, shields of bliss, tempests
of storm-filled, delighted feeling and, suddenly, solitary
mirrors: gathering their own out-streamed beauty
back into their faces again.

Using natural metaphors that encapsulate *'there-ness'*, energy-filled presence, and fertility, he tries to describe their favoured status, their completeness, yet creative power. They are *pollen of flowering godhead*, and there is a relevant statement of the open secret of Egyptian sculptures in a Letter of 1914, their enigmatic mysteriousness which is nevertheless perfectly revealed in their solidity and assertive polished surfaces. They are both inscrutable and revealing to the initiate. Rilke writes that he *'cannot recall the smile of the Egyptian gods without thinking of the word pollen,'* a word which expresses openly Nature's secret of sexuality which is also the hidden phallic secret of clothed human beings. And the angels are *solitary mirrors* that gather their beauty back into their own faces, an image of Rilke's desire for, and love of, solitude, and his self-contained, perhaps self-centred, even narcissistic, nature.

For we, when we feel, evaporate: oh, we
breathe ourselves out and away: from ember to ember,
yielding us fainter fragrance. Then someone may say to us:
'Yes, you are in my blood, the room, the Spring-time
is filling with you'..... What use is that: they cannot hold us,
we vanish inside and around them. And those who are beautiful,
oh, who holds them back? Appearance, endlessly, stands up,
in their face, and goes by. Like dew from the morning grass,
what is ours rises from us, like the heat
from a dish that is warmed. O smile: where? O upward gaze:
new, warm, vanishing wave of the heart - :oh, we are that.

By contrast with the Angel, we human beings are transient and incomplete. We breathe away our existence like incense among embers, and in relationship our identity even if grasped for a moment is unstable and vanishes from the mind of the other. All appearance, even that of beauty, is evanescent and flows by, and our being evaporates like dew from the grass, or rises and dissipates like heat from a dish. The smile and the gaze, those two key attributes of Dante's Beatrice in the Divine Comedy, the means by which we communicate deeply with others, betray us as both fleeting and unstable, both are evidence of process rather than permanence.

Does the cosmic space,

we dissolve into, taste of us then? Do the Angels

really only take back what is theirs, what has streamed out of them,

or is there sometimes, as if by an oversight, something

of our being, as well? Are we as mingled with their

features, as there is vagueness in the faces

of pregnant women? They do not see it in the swirling

return to themselves. (How should they see it?)

In which case, since our being streams away from us, does an element of that being sometimes merge with the Angels' existence, even if they are unconscious of it, as the faces of pregnant women may unconsciously reveal the vague presence of another being, another life, within them?

Lovers, if they knew how, might utter

strange things in night air. Since it seems

everything hides us. Look, trees exist; houses,

we live in, still stand. Only we

pass everything by, like an exchange of air.

And all is at one, in keeping us secret, half out of

shame perhaps, half out of inexpressible hope.

Rilke invokes the lovers, who hold an inward, in-turned reality between them. They might present a clue: because everything conceals our inner consciousness, and hides us. We pass through everything, like a spiritual breath of air. Everything conceals us, the creatures mid-way between animal and angel, and therefore subjects of shame or hope.

Lovers, each satisfied in the other, I ask
you about us. You grasp yourselves. Have you a sign?
Look, it happens to me, that at times my hands
become aware of each other, or that my worn face
hides itself in them. That gives me a slight
sensation. But who would dare to exist only for that?
You, though, who grow in the other's delight
until, overwhelmed, they beg:
'No more' -: you, who under your hands
grow richer like vintage years of the vine:
who sometimes vanish, because the other
has so gained the ascendancy: I ask you of us. I know
you touch so blissfully because the caress withholds,
because the place you cover so tenderly
does not disappear: because beneath it you feel
pure duration. So that you promise eternity
almost, from the embrace

Lovers represent the extremes of material, sensual delight, the bliss of physical relationship, which in miniature we feel, in stimulation, when we touch our hands together or clasp our face between them, a slight sensation, but insufficient to justify existing. The lovers' embrace gives a timeless, eternal sensation to the physical, so that the place of their touching seems for an instant beyond the ephemeral and evanescent, and is pure existence, the moment, the now, pure being, pure duration. '*Simply beneath his hand, this place lasts, is*', says Rilke of the lover in a letter of 1913.

And yet, when you've endured
the first terrible glances, and the yearning at windows,
and the first walk together, just once, through the garden:
Lovers, are you the same? When you raise yourselves
one to another's mouth, and hang there – sip against sip:
O, how strangely the drinker then escapes from their action.

Nevertheless, love itself is ritual and becomes process, and lovers fail to maintain the eternity of the initial relationship beyond the first, glance, desire, walk, kiss, sexual encounter. Physical love too is evanescent. The fleeting intuition of eternity slips away.

Weren't you amazed by the caution of human gesture
on Attic steles? Weren't love and departure
laid so lightly on shoulders, they seemed to be made
of other matter than ours? Think of the hands
how they rest without weight, though there is power in the torso.
Those self-controlled ones know, through that: so much is ours,
this is us, to touch our own selves so: the gods
may bear down more heavily on us. But that is the gods' affair.

Rilke recalls the restraint of the figures on Attic funeral monuments, the steles, where the gestures are light and constrained, weightless and gentle, and suggests that such restraint is more appropriate to us than sexual ecstasy because it can be sustained by our modest level of strength and power. 'I really believe', he wrote in a letter of 1912, 'I sometimes get as far as to express my whole heart's impulse, without loss or fatality, in laying my hand gently on a shoulder'. Yet we moderns, unlike the Greeks, cannot find adequate symbols outside us to reflect the conscious life within us.

If only we too could discover a pure, contained
human place, a strip of fruitful land of our own,
between river and stone! For our own heart exceeds us,
even as theirs did. And we can no longer
gaze after it into images, that soothe it, or into
godlike bodies, where it restrains itself more completely.

Rilke echoes Goethe's search for the Classical, in the second part of Faust, in this search for a fruitful land, and also recalls his visits to the Nile in 1911. Our hearts, our longing, our capacity for feeling, memory and expectation, exceed our grasp, our ability to achieve, but we can no longer create Greek forms to soothe us nor believe in the gods as a visible example to us of classical restraint.

The second Elegy has shown us our immediate limitations, our place in the spectrum of consciousness, and the inability of the physical, even in sexual delight, to reach the timeless, while the Classical examples of a more formal and moderate restraint have passed beyond us, and are no longer easily realisable in modernity. The third Elegy sees Rilke delving deeper into the human condition, as he explores the themes of sub-conscious impulse, male sexuality and childhood. He considers what links us to our ancestors, and hints at the inescapable biological and genetic reality of human beings.

THE THIRD ELEGY

To sing the beloved is one thing, another, oh,
that hidden guilty river-god of the blood.
What does he know, himself, of that lord of desire, her young lover, whom she
knows distantly, who often out of his solitariness,
before the girl soothed him, often, as if she did not exist,
held up, dripping, from what unknowable depths,
his godhead, oh, rousing the night to endless uproar?

Beneath the relationship of love, lies the reality of sexuality, in particular here male sexuality. The conscious mind even of the male lover is ignorant of the sub-conscious power of the instincts.

O Neptune of the blood, O his trident of terrors.
O the dark storm-wind from his chest, out of the twisted conch.

The god within, the genetic basis of our being, is still powerful in our psyches, and capable of usurping reason and abolishing moderation, in favour of an intensity which is in itself terrifying, as it calls into question our habitual and stable selves, our familiar conscious world.

Hear, how the night becomes thinned-out and hollow. You, stars,
is it not from you that the lover's joy in the beloved's
face rises? Does he not gain his innermost insight,
into her face's purity, from the pure stars?

The lover's cry of instinct from the twisted conch of his being rises into the night, which grows fluted and hollowed in sympathy. That cry rises to the stars which echo to us the purity and light which shines, for a lover, in the face of the beloved girl. The universe therefore inspires the human, and offsets instinct with permanence, the tempest with night and its feminine soothing calm. Rilke's thought moves backwards to childhood and the mother, who is also the universal mother, Nature.

It was not you, alas, not his mother
that bent the arc of his brow into such expectation.
Not for you, girl, feeling his presence, not for you,
did his lips curve into a more fruitful expression.
Do you truly think that your light entrance
rocked him so, you who wander like winds at dawn?
You terrified his heart, that's so: but more ancient terrors
plunged into him with the impetus of touching.

There are deeper things than visible experience beneath behaviour and being. Touch, sensation, leads us backwards into primeval arenas where the species once existed. They exist behind and beneath, and also above rationality, in the spaces of the universe and of our selves. Sexuality, like birth and death, is one of the primitive experiences that we have sanitised, and even abused and exploited, but which still connects us to the origins of our existence.

Call him...you can't quite call him away from that dark companion.
Of course he wants to, and does, escape: relieved, winning
his way into your secret heart, and takes on, and begins himself.

The female here calls the male away from the instincts (Note Rilke's view of sexuality, remarkably liberated for his era, as we see in his letters and elsewhere, but still conditioned, as regards woman, by his social context)

Did he ever begin himself, though?
Mother you made his littleness: you were the one who began him:
to you he was new, you hung the friendly world
over new eyes, and defended him from what was strange.
Oh where are the years when you simply repelled
the surging void for him, with your slight form?
You hid so much from him then: you made the suspect room
harmless at night, from your heart filled with refuge
mixed a more human space with his spaces of night.
Not in the darkness, no, in your nearer being
you placed the light, and it shone as if out of friendship.
There wasn't a single creaking you couldn't explain with a smile,
as if you had long known when the floor would do so....
And he heard you and was soothed. Your being
was so tenderly potent: his fate there stepped,
tall and cloaked, behind the wardrobe, and his restless future,
so easily delayed, fitted the folds of the curtain.

This straightforward passage depicts the mother shielding the child from the realities of adult existence. In childhood our fate is concealed, it is potent in that all possibilities are open, and can seem like a hiatus before a second birth into the wider world. There is a rhapsody on this theme of the protecting mother in Rilke's *The Notebooks of Malte Laurids Brigge*, the mother who *'in the night had the courage to be this silence for the frightened child, dying of fear... and keep the monstrous behind you and are entirely before it, not like a curtain it can raise here and there....as if you had arrived far ahead of anything that might yet happen, and had behind you only your swift arrival, your eternal arc, the flight of your love.'* The mother causes fate to fade into the background while protective love creates its 'temporary' stillness in eternity.

And he himself, as he lay there, relieved,
dissolving a sweetness, of your gentle creation,
under his sleepy eyelids, into the sleep he had tasted - :
seemed protected.....But inside: who could hinder,
prevent, the primal flood inside him?
Ah, there was little caution in the sleeper: sleeping,
but dreaming, but fevered: what began there!
How, new, fearful, he was tangled
in ever-spreading tendrils of inner event:
already twisted in patterns, in strangling growths,
among prowling bestial forms. How he gave himself to it -. Loved.

The external arc of childhood conceals the complex inner development of emotions and thought. Rilke gives an autobiographical sensation to this description, as if it were contemplating the childhood of this immensely inward and self-centred poet.

Loved his inward world, his inner wilderness,
that first world within, on whose mute overthrow
his heart stood, newly green. Loved. Relinquished it, went on,
through his own roots, to the vast fountain
where his little birth was already outlived. Lovingly
went down into more ancient bloodstreams, into ravines
where Horror lay, still gorged on his forefathers. And every
Terror knew him, winked, like an informant.
Yes, Dread smiled........

Development in some sense recapitulates the early history of the species and the child in the inward world descends to the primeval roots of sensation, feeling and awareness, including our deepest fears and loathing. Rilke wrote of the history of the species as: *'a primeval forest whose floor we never reach, because it stands endlessly, layer on layer, on what has been overthrown, an apparition on the back of downfall.'* This idea of recapitulation is further extended.

Seldom
have you smiled so tenderly, mothers. How could he
help loving what smiled at him. Before you
he loved it, since, while you carried him,
it was dissolved in the waters, that render the embryo light.

Rilke gives a touching description of the child bathed in the eternal smile of the maternal, as the embryo was bathed in just such a maternal flow in the womb.

See, we don't love like flowers, in a
single year: when we love, an ancient
sap rises in our arms. O, girls,
this: that we loved inside us, not one to come, but
the immeasurable seething: not a single child,
but the fathers: resting on our depths
like the rubble of mountains: the dry river-beds
of those who were mothers - : the whole
silent landscape under a clouded or
clear destiny - : girls, this came before you.

Rilke completes the image of the universal consciousness of the species as an ancient landscape that will re-appear in the tenth and last Elegy. He forges here the connection between the developing child and the generations of the dead, not merely the living and the unborn, but rather that *immeasurable seething* of all the generations past and to come. Note that the metaphor of *dry river-beds* echoes his poem Tombs of the Courtesans. Thus, the child contains within itself the past and future potential of the species.

And you yourself, how could you know — that you
stirred up primordial time in your lover. What feelings
welled up from lost lives. What
women hated you there. What sinister men
you roused up in his young veins. Dead
children wanted you.....

Rilke creates the atmosphere of the double-realm by mingling the dead and the living. The emotions and responses of the dead are also ours. Our perceptions and feelings were, and, in the eternal moment of the whole, are also theirs. Rilke fuses both realms completely in the last phrase...*Dead children wanted you*...where the adjective places the living person addressed into the vanished moment of being of children now dead.

O, gently, gently,
show him with love a confident daily task - lead him
near to the Garden, give him what outweighs
those nights........
                    Be in him..............

Rilke stresses the need of man for woman, for her espousal of the confident daily task lovingly performed which she can demonstrate to him, or lead him to. This at first sight seems a dated concept of the female role, though clearly such a role remains one dimension of female existence, but note how the last phrase *Be in him,* seeks to fuse male and female, the male absorbing a female element to achieve wholeness. It would certainly be wrong to write Rilke off as merely possessing a male view of life, rather he tries to get beyond the distinction and embrace the continuum of human experience. He wrote in a letter: '*some day there will be girls and women whose name will no longer signify merely an opposite of the masculine, but something in itself, something that makes one think not of any complement and limit, but only of life and existence: the feminine human being.* This humanity of woman '*will come to light when she has stripped off the conventions of mere femininity in the mutations of her outward status, and those men who do not yet feel it approaching today will be surprised and struck by it*'. And finally he stressed that the experience of love would be forced to change also '*from the ground up, reshaped into a relation of one human being to another, no longer of man to woman.*'

The third Elegy has exposed our deeper condition of being, our continuity with the past, and past consciousness, recapitulated in childhood development, and expressed later in sexuality where the feminine and masculine elements need to be fused to create the whole life. The fourth Elegy now returns to a theme touched on in the first Elegy, our innate inner conflicts, the divided nature of mind that feels the pull of irreconcilable goals and prevents us from resting absorbed in that between-world experienced in childhood, where the world and the toy or the world and the game fuse into pure play, and awareness is rapture. We are out of harmony with instinctive life and therefore out of harmony with death also.

THE FOURTH ELEGY

O trees of life, O when are you wintering?
We are not unified. We have no instincts
like those of migratory birds. Useless, and late,
we force ourselves, suddenly, onto the wind,
and fall down to an indifferent lake.
We realise flowering and fading together.
And somewhere lions still roam. Never knowing,
as long as they have their splendour, of any weakness.

We are *trees of life*, but we do not contain the reality of the seasons within us, the budding, flowering, leafing, shedding and over-wintering of the deciduous trees in nature. We lack the unity of the cyclical world, the instincts of migratory birds that urge them into congregation and flight. We fail to recognise the signals of change and departure until too late and then throw ourselves into circumstances inappropriate to our inner selves. Our flowering and fading seem virtually simultaneous, both in our mental processes and also in our physical duration. Yet other creatures, lions for example, seem fully integrated into their lives, never foreseeing, in their splendour, their own illness or death, launching themselves into life fully rather than hanging back, in fear of it.

We, though, while we are intent on one thing, wholly,
feel the loss of some other. Enmity
is our neighbour.

Rilke goes on to diagnose the human condition, and its many limitations, as he sees it. We humans have divided goals, and while trying to complete one task we are already thinking of another, our inability to possess both in the one moment causing a sense of loss and frustration. Conflict and an enmity between goals are always with us, and circumstances may seem hostile simply because of our inability to read life's depths.

Aren't lovers
always arriving at boundaries, each of the other,
who promised distance, hunting, and home?

Lovers too while promising each other eternity and the boundlessness of a sense of space, pursuit and resolution (physically in the sexual act but mentally in many other ways) that the hunting creatures, like the lions, possess, also meet boundaries in each other formed by non-acceptance, unwillingness, difference and non-comprehension.

And when, for the sketch of a moment,
a contrasting background is carefully prepared
so that we can see it: then this is clear
to us. We do not know the contours
of feeling, only what forms it from outside.

And in fact we understand our feelings only by coming to see them as a result of the external forces which created them, as a contrasting background highlights a foreground contour. In this sense emotions, like language are social rather than innate. We call forth the correct feeling or phrase from the repertoire of feelings and words we know in response to the social context. The background provokes our foreground reaction.

Who has not sat, scared, before his heart's curtain?
It drew itself up: the scenery was of Departure.
Easy to comprehend.

Possessed by fear of the future, and of death, human beings wait to see the play of their own being acted out on the inner mental stage, Rilke suggests, perhaps betraying the nature of his own specific psyche, that of the observer and voyeur, gripped by a certain passivity in relationship to life and others. And the play such a psyche sees will always be of scenes of departure because the moment is always slipping from our hands, our present is always vanishing beneath our feet into the past, and our future is present before we know it, and past before we can grasp it. Relevant references here are to Baudelaire's poem *The Inquisitive Man's* Dream, where the whole feel of this stage-set in the mind is contained, and also to Heinrich von Kleist's *On the Marionette Theatre* (1810) a work which Rilke admired.

The familiar garden
swaying a little: then the dancer appeared.
Not him. Enough! However lightly he moves
he is in costume, and turns into a citizen,
and goes through the kitchen into his house.

What appears on the stage however is the same habitual and conventional actor, who is our own self, rather than the something essential, fresh and eternal that we long to see as our destiny; our future: a fate both open and infinite. We seem only half-completed to ourselves. We fulfil roles, but badly, being inward and individual as well as outward and social.

I don't want these half-completed masks,
rather the Doll. That is complete. I will
suffer its shell, its wire, its face
of mere appearance.

A doll or puppet would be more complete, external. Even though mere shell and appearance it would fulfil the role more absolutely.

Here. I am waiting.
Even if the lights go out, even if someone
says to me: 'No more' - , even if emptiness
reaches me as a grey draught of air from the stage,
even if none of my silent forefathers
sits by me any more, not one woman,
not even the boy [p. 220] with the brown, squinting, eyes.
I'll still be here. One can always watch.

So, frustrated by incompleteness, the poet waits, even if the waiting is a time of emptiness, even if the dead do not return to him within, as modes of his consciousness, not even beloved women, the feminine aspects of life, not even the early-dead, symbols of eternity, in this case Egon von Rilke, his cousin, who died in childhood at the age of seven, of whom Rilke wrote: '*the sadness and helplessness of childhood is embodied for me in his form.*' One can always be a voyeur. One can always watch life, and one's inner self, in hope.

Am I not right? You, to whom life tasted
so bitter, father, tasting mine,
that first clouded infusion of my necessities,
you kept on tasting, as I grew,
and preoccupied by the after-taste
of such a strange future, searched my misted gaze –
you, my father, who since you were dead, have often
been anxious within my innermost hopes,
and giving up calm, the kingdoms of calm
the dead own, for my bit of fate,
am I not right?

Rilke invokes the shade of his anxious father, an inner spiritual companion, as witness to his vision, and the appropriateness of patience.

And you women, am I not right,
who would love me for that small beginning
of love, for you, that I always turned away from,
because the space of your faces changed,
as I loved, into cosmic space,
where you no longer existed

And he invokes beloved women, with whom he failed to establish deeper relationships because he saw only the infinite emptiness of cosmic space beyond them and through them until they ceased to exist for him. Here Rilke is confessing to his own self-centredness, his own solipsism as regards the world of other human beings, his own inability to be satisfied by the human:

......When I feel
like waiting in front of the puppet theatre, no,
rather gazing at it, so intently, that at last,
to balance my gaze, an Angel must come
and take part, dragging the puppets on high.
Angel and Doll: then there's a play at last.

By waiting he believes the Angel must arrive, that concept of the transforming powers. By gazing, through thought and poetry, into the world he anticipates that his thought and art will be transformed to a higher plane, where the human will be mediated between the Angel and the Puppet, the more than human and the less than human, the wholly internal and the wholly external. Then....

Then what we endlessly separate,
merely by being, comes together. Then at last
from our seasons here, the orbit
of all change emerges. Over and above us,
then, the Angel plays.

Then the fragmented might become whole, the complete cycle of our changing life might be visible, and actual. The Angel, creative transforming consciousness, would then play with being, with our being also, in the way the dancing god Siva does in the religion of India, creating and destroying worlds, species, individuals, the phases of our life, moments even, in an endless rhythm, for the creative force in us manifests itself as play, on many levels. When it is truly whole the intellect plays with life, beyond fear or hope, in the intensity of our gaze and our games.

See the dying
must realise that what we do here
is nothing, how full of pretext it all is,
nothing in itself.

Here, Rilke condemns the seeming pointlessness of human activity, the pretexts that clothe our efforts, and their ultimate impermanence and therefore emptiness. This is close to the Buddhist concept of *maya*, the sea of perceptual illusion. Death, Rilke would maintain, gives life greater significance, because consciousness of it leads to whole vision, and complete transformation.

O hours of childhood,
when, behind the images, there was more
than the past, and in front of us was not the future.
We were growing, it's true, and sometimes urged that
we soon grew up, half for the sake
of those others who had nothing but their grown-up-ness.
And were, yet, on our own, happy
with Timelessness, and stood there,
in the space between world and plaything,
at a point that from first beginnings
had been marked out for pure event.

The world of the child in contrast to that of adults has moments in eternity where the past and future are absent from consciousness in the intensity of gaze, or play. The child exists in the space between world and plaything. Rilke, in his essay on Dolls of 1914, asks us to remember one of those toys, those things of childhood, which first focused attention on the other, even though an inanimate other, some *'forgotten object that was ready to signify everything.*' He suggests the child experiences *'through its existence, its humdrum appearance, its final breakage, and enigmatic exit, all that is human, right into the depths of death.'* What the child experiences, and the adult finds so hard to recover, is unconditional being, in moments of intensity which for the child are casual and everyday, those instances of conscious awareness that Rilke calls *pure event*. In a letter of 1903 he praised the hours of loneliness '*vast inner loneliness*' from which the child regards the alien adult world it fails to comprehend, because those hours enshrine a precious and '*wise lack of understanding*' that remains connected to pure event. And elsewhere, in a letter of 1924, he describes the intuition '*that at some deeper cross-section of this pyramid of consciousness, mere being could become an event, the inviolable presence and simultaneity of everything that we on the normal higher level of consciousness are permitted to experience only as entropy.*' Rilke now questions whether we see or portray childhood that is, portray ourselves, fully if we ignore the facts of our mortal fate, our ultimate death.

> *Who shows a child, just as they are? Who sets it*
> *in its constellation, and gives the measure*
> *of distance into its hand? Who makes a child's death*
> *out of grey bread, that hardens, - or leaves it*
> *inside its round mouth like the core*
> *of a shining apple? Killers are*
> *easy to grasp. But this: death,*
> *the whole of death, before life,*
> *to hold it so softly, and not live in anger,*
> *cannot be expressed.*

And who then depicts a child as it really exists, truly places it within the eternity of cosmic space it inhabits for a while, and at the right depth or height relative to our adult world? To do so would require us, like a painter, to show death, which is the child's ultimate fate as child or adult, our own unavoidable destiny, incipient within its childhood being (something we no doubt fear to do because of the ill-luck associated with such a depiction). It would be necessary to portray that death, symbolise it perhaps in the grey uneaten piece of hardened bread on a plate that lurks in the soft freshly-baked loaf, or like the core of an apple hidden within the ripe fruit, left uneaten within the child's mouth. It is easy to grasp the concept of murder, the destruction of a child and the life it represents, much harder to consciously realise that death is there from the start, even before life begins, and then in looking at the child, at its innocence, be able to hold that concept as it were in the cupped hands, softly and gently, without bitterness or anger at the human predicament. In a conceptual sense to rehearse that thought within the mind is to commit a mental murder, to destroy the being the child represents, through the realisation of death, without intending destruction or even wishing harm. The adult destroys childhood with every breath, unintentionally, and without malice, merely through being what adulthood represents, and merely by the child being what it is, innocence and pure event.

The fourth Elegy then has emphasised the divided nature of the adult consciousness, and contrasted it with childhood. It has suggested the emptiness of the role-playing of adulthood, and the need to summon the Angel of transforming consciousness, which exists at times in the child's games and gaze. And Rilke has suggested that we need to see death within life, and life within death, as the double-realm, in order to understand what we are, and how we might become. The fifth Elegy finds another symbolic stage for human life, in the circus acrobats derived from a Picasso painting and his own life in Paris, and contemplates what it would take to make such activity as ours meaningful, perhaps in the person of lovers.

THE FIFTH ELEGY

But who are they, tell me, these Travellers [p. 220], even more

transient than we are ourselves, urgently, from their earliest days,

wrung out for whom — to please whom,

by a never-satisfied will? Yet it wrings them,

bends them, twists them, and swings them,

throws them, and catches them again: as if from oiled

more slippery air, so they land

on the threadbare carpet, worn by their continual

leaping, this carpet

lost in the universe.

Stuck on like a plaster, as if the suburban

sky had wounded the earth there.

The travellers are the acrobats of Picasso's painting *Family of Saltimbanques* (1905), which Rilke was familiar with from his stay in Munich, in the summer and autumn of 1915, living in a house where the painting hung, a painting *'in which there is so much Paris, that, for moments, I forget.'* He describes elsewhere a troupe of circus people led by Père Rollin he saw in Paris in 1907, whose aspect also passes into the Elegy. They are versions of ourselves, we human beings, only they are even more transient wanderers, moving their act from square to square of the city, as we are driven on by some unfulfilled external expectation or eternally-disappointed will to perform our actions, on the threadbare carpet of our planet, lost in the universe, stuck-on here to the Earth, like some unfortunate wound rather than intrinsic or natural.

And scarcely there,

upright, there and revealed: the great
capital letter of Being.........and already the ever-returning
grasp wrings the strongest of men again, in jest,
as King August the Strong would crush
a tin plate.

The grouping on the left of Picasso's painting forms a scarcely delineated D for *Dasein* or Being, while gravity and time make a mockery of the strength of even the strongest man, as King Augustus of Poland could crush a pewter plate in his hand.

Ah, and around this
centre, the rose of watching
flowers and un-flowers. Round this
stamp, this pistil, caught in the pollen
of its own flowering, fertilised
again to a shadow-fruit of disinterest,
their never-conscious, seeming-to-smile, disinterest,
gleaming lightly, on surface thinness.

The spectators of our actions come and go, flower and un-flower, caught by a passing interest, yet fruiting only into a mild false-smile of polite disinterest.

There, the withered, wrinkled lifter,
an old man, only a drummer now,
shrunk in his massive hide, as though it had once
contained two men, and one was already
lying there in the churchyard, and the other had survived him,
deaf, and sometimes a little
confused in his widowed skin.

Our age is represented there, reduced as Père Rollin was to drumming
instead of acrobatics.

And the young one, the man, as if he were son of a neck
and a nun: taut and erectly filled
with muscle and simple-mindedness.

And our youth: physical and naïve.

O you,
that a sorrow, that was still small,
once received as a plaything, in one of its
long convalescences......

And our childhood:

You, who fall, with the thud
that only fruit knows, unripe,
a hundred times a day from the tree of mutually
built-up movement (that, swifter than water,
in a few moments, shows spring, summer and autumn),
fall, and impact on the grave:
sometimes, in half-pauses, a loving look tries
to rise from your face towards your seldom
affectionate mother: but it loses itself in your body,
whose surface consumes the shy
scarcely-attempted look......And again
the man is clapping his hands for your leap, and before
a pain can become more distinct, close to your
constantly racing heart, a burning grows in the soles of your feet,
its source, before a few quick tears rush bodily into your eyes.

Our childhood repeats the species in recapitulation, time after time, from birth to the grave, from the leap of the child acrobat to his return to earth. And during our leap of life, our arc of being we sometimes look almost lovingly towards the Earth, our mother, as the little boy looks in the painting towards the woman at the right, our mother which is seldom kind to us, which stings our feet with gravity in our return from our efforts to evade it, and yet whose surface we continue to leap from again and again, driven on by the urge of development through adulthood towards old age, swallowing our sadness at our transience and embracing activity which only adds to our pain and sorrow.

And yet, blindly,
that smile........

Yet that loving look, that sly almost vanishing smile, directed at our mother, the Earth, at our deeper origins, is nevertheless precious:

Angel! O, gather it, pluck it, that small-flowered healing herb.
Make a vase, keep it safe! Place it among those joys not yet
open to us: on a lovely urn,
praise it, with flowery, swirling, inscription:
'Subrisio Saltat: the Saltimbanque's smile'

...worthy enough for the Angel of transformation to pluck it like a healing herb, a balm for the spirit, a future joy resulting from transformation, and preserve it in an urn inscribed, *The Acrobat's Smile.*

You, then, beloved,
you, that the loveliest delights
silently over-leapt. Perhaps
your frills are happy for you –
or the green metallic silk,
over your firm young breasts,
feels itself endlessly pampered, and needing nothing.
You, market fruit of serenity
laid out, endlessly, on all the quivering balance scales,
publicly, beneath the shoulders.

And the nubile girl is also a performance, woman is also exhibited, in this same ritual display of human activity symbolised here by the circus acrobats.

Where, oh where is the place — I carry it in my heart —
where they were still far from capable, still fell away
from each other, like coupling animals, not yet
ready for pairing: -
where the weights are still heavy:
where the plates still topple
from their vainly twirling
sticks.......

Where, Rilke, asks is the reality of our being which this facile, skilled display of habitual, ritual activity masks. Where is the place where the striving (of poetic effort, for example) is still actual and vital and not mere empty performance? We humans need that continual striving, that continual transformation which re-makes the world and makes it real and whole, and perhaps there is a clue in the regions of non-performance, before the work is matured, before our lives are 'finished'.

And, suddenly, in this troublesome nowhere, suddenly,
the unsayable point where the pure too-little
is changed incomprehensibly -, altered
into that empty too-much.
Where the many-placed calculation
is exactly resolved.

Where is the moment, among difficulties, those agents of reality, where the insufficient suddenly becomes sufficient, and yet before it reduces to stale repetition, hollow excess, dwindles to that place where the complex sum is resolved, and the calculation reduces to a mere zero?

Squares: O square in Paris, endless show-place,
where the milliner, Madame Lamort,
winds and twists the restless trails of the earth,
endless ribbons, into new
bows, frills, flowers, rosettes, artificial fruits – all
falsely coloured, - for winter's
cheap hats of destiny.

Reduces to the endless city squares where we, the acrobats, perform, reduces to the indifferent market-place where Madame Death decks us out in the artificial and transient fashions that decorate our trivial and worthless fates.

Angel: if there were a place we know nothing of, and there,
on some unsayable carpet, lovers revealed
what here they could never master, their high daring
figures of heart's flight,
their towers of desire, their ladders,
long since standing where there was no ground, leaning,
trembling, on each other – and mastered them,
in front of the circle of watchers, the countless, soundless dead:

If only there was, somewhere, a place where the lovers who fail to achieve lasting inward transformation in life, who teeter on the ladders and towers of relationship, could master the flights of love, as the acrobats of the everyday, we humans, have mastered our empty performance. And if only that could be done in front of the past generations (and such performance carries erotic, voyeuristic sexual overtones as well as Rilke's other spiritual meanings), the dead who watch in our consciousness, then:

Would these not fling their last, ever-saved,
ever-hidden, unknown to us, eternally
valid coins of happiness in front of the finally
truly smiling pair on the silent
carpet?

...would not that audience shower coins of happiness (like the coins thrown traditionally at weddings in various countries, and the coins thrown to the acrobats) in front of the fulfilled couple, would we not achieve transformation of our inner reality, and not merely the empty performance of our external one?

The fifth Elegy has expressed Rilke's condemnation of the hollowness of our worldly lives (it is well to bear in mind throughout the Elegies this negative approach to external social reality, and the reader must decide on its validity. Is Rilke's diagnosis true, or is it coloured too much by his own psyche and character?), and utilises the symbolism of the street acrobats to express the ritual, and facile skills of everyday existence. The suggestion, or hope, is that somehow there might be a way of uniting the realms of the dead and the living in a more fruitful, achieved performance than our habitual one, a greater wholeness. The sixth Elegy returns to the Hero, mentioned in the first Elegy, who like the unrequited lovers, and the early-departed might offer a key to our internal transformation, to a greater and fuller life. These three groups, or four if we include the lovers of the previous elegy, stand at the edge of our external life, pointing towards the internal, and as aspects of the transient pointing towards the infinite. (A note to the reader: it may be wise not to assume that the realm of dead has some objective reality, beyond the world of living, in Rilke's scheme. That may have been his view, but he is much more interested in bringing both realms within, in a transformation of consciousness. Is Rilke religious in any conventional sense? Does he believe in an objective after-life? A caution to the reader not to be too sure: equally, to regard the Angels as concept rather than external reality is more helpful in understanding Rilke's direction than not.)

THE SIXTH ELEGY

Fig-tree, for such a long time now, there has been meaning for me,
in the way you almost wholly omit to flower
and urge your pure secret, unheralded,
into the early, resolute fruit.
Like the jet of a fountain, your arched bough
drives the sap downward, then up: and it leaps from its sleep
barely waking, into the bliss of its sweetest achievement.
See: like the god into the swan

The fig-tree fruits two or three times a year, the fruit forming rapidly. Rilke employs it as a symbol, with sexual overtones, of the life that comes to early fruition and achievement, leaping into its completion, like the divine Zeus taking on the form of a swan to plunge towards his fulfilment with the mortal Leda. The fruit, the achievement, is more vital for this tree than its flowering.

..........We, though, linger,
ah, our pride is in flowering, and, already betrayed,
we reach the late core of our final fruit.

We humans, in contrast, take all our pride in flowering, and we reach death, that core of the fruit, to use the image from the end of the fourth Elegy, almost before we have ripened. Life betrays us into death.

In a few the urge to action rises so powerfully,
that they are already waiting and glowing with their heart's fullness
when the temptation to flower, like the mild night air,
touches their tender mouths, touches their eyelids:
heroes perhaps, and those chosen to vanish prematurely,
in whom Death the gardener wove different veins.

The heroes, perhaps, and the early-dead are exceptions, beginning their flowering with a sense of ripeness already within them. They are fruits that Death, the gardener (a chilling image, a variant of Death the Reaper of traditional iconography) has singled out for a premature harvest.

These plunge ahead: they go before their own smile,
like the team of horses in the slightly
hollowed-out relief of Karnak's victorious pharaoh.

They are almost ahead of their own fate, plunging toward and through it, icons of the too-early lost. Rilke is reminded of his visit to '*the incomprehensible temple-world of Karnak*' in Egypt in 1911, and the battle-scenes carved on the pillars in the Temple of Amun, depicting the conquering pharaohs in their swift chariots.

The hero is strangely close to those who died young. Lasting
doesn't contain him. Being is his ascent: he moves on,
time and again, to enter the changed constellation
his risk entails. Few could find him there. But
Destiny, that darkly hides us, suddenly inspired,
sings him into the tempest of his onrushing world.
I hear no one like him. All at once I am pierced
by his darkened sound carried on streaming air.

The hero, like the early-dead, is marked by movement towards his end rather than duration or permanence. Achilles' end is already foreseen in the opening movements of the Iliad, the hero is doomed, fated, singled out by destiny and already in motion, even as he skulks in his hut. Though he avoids the conflict the epic is waiting only for him. Few can be heroes, and though most of our fates are obscure and hidden his is celebrated and sung by Destiny, as he rides the storm-wind of action.

> *Then, how gladly I would hide from the yearning: O if I,*
> *if I were a boy, and might come to it still, and sit,*
> *propped on the future's arms, and reading about Samson,*
> *how his mother first bore nothing, and then all.*

There is a suggestion here that Rilke sees the poet's role as heroic, and his own life as fated, or at least that he yearned for such a role, but would prefer to recapitulate the security of childhood, of books and his own propped arms, to read about heroism rather than perform it. In the Biblical story, Samson's mother, the wife of Manoah, is barren and then bears the hero, after a prophecy delivered to her by an angel. (Judges: 13)

> *Was he not a hero already, O mother, in you, did not*
> *his imperious choice begin inside you?*
> *Thousands seethed in the womb and willed to be him,*
> *but see: he grasped and let go, chose and achieved.*
> *And if he shattered pillars, it was when he burst*
> *out of the world of your flesh into the narrower world,*
> *where he went on choosing, achieving. O mothers of heroes,*

In a poetic conceit, Rilke imagines the hero already choosing his own birth, selecting himself and his fate from the many selves and fates represented by the eggs and fertilising sperm in the womb. Samson's shattering of the pillars of the Philistines (Judges:16) is a recapitulation of his bursting out of the womb into life, though then it is a bursting out of life into heroic death, which completes the whole of his fate.

O sources of ravening rivers! Ravines into which

weeping girls have plunged

from the high heart's edge, future offerings to the son.

Because, whenever the hero stormed through the stations of love,

each heartbeat, meant for him, lifting him onward,

he turned away, stood at the end of the smiles, someone other.

The hero rushes on towards his goal, and so has no time for the fulfilment of relationship (Is this Rilke arguing the case to himself, justifying himself, his own failures of relationship?). The hero is turned away from the world and already intensely involved with something else, a greater (or is it a lesser? The reader must be alert to Rilke's seductive flow) reality than temporal love.

The sixth Elegy has celebrated the hero, through reflection on whose junction of life and death we might transform consciousness. The seventh is a celebration of transformation itself, and therefore of our conscious life which makes that transformation of the external world possible, and allows us the possibility of integration and wholeness.

THE SEVENTH ELEGY

Wooing, no longer: wooing will not be the form of your
cry, voice that's outgrown it: true, you would cry pure as a bird,
when the season lifts him, the ascending one, almost forgetting
that he is a suffering creature, and not just a solitary heart
that it flings into brightness, to intimate heavens.

R ilke returns to the unuttered opening cry of the first Elegy, a stifled inward cry of wooing that he considers no longer appropriate to his new knowledge. A voice that has now outgrown the simple desire for consolation and help should not seek to sing with the voice of a person wooing the Other or the Angel. True song is in fact not desire, but Being, says one of the Sonnets to Orpheus (I:3) Even though, if he did cry out, the cry of wooing he uttered would be, like the pure cry of the bird, almost forgetful of our human condition of suffering and transience, our solitariness within life, where the Other is always something beyond us, separated from us by a boundary, of mind or flesh, matter or mystery. *'The bird has a special feeling of trust in the external world'*, Rilke wrote, and we feel that it *'does not distinguish between its heart and the world's'*. (Letter, 1914) True song is even beyond that pure bird voice.

Like him,
you also, would be wooing no less — so that, still invisible,
some girl would sense you, the silent one, in whom a reply
slowly wakes and grows warm, as she listens —
the glowing feeling mated to your daring feeling.

The voice of that wooing would have the effect, like the bird's, of wakening response in a potential mate.

Oh and the Spring-time would comprehend — there is no place
that would not echo its voice of proclamation.
First the tiny questioning piping, that a purely affirmative day
surrounds more deeply with heightened stillness.
Then up the stairway, the stairway of calling, up to
the dreamed-of temple of future - : then the trill, fountain
that in its rising jet already anticipates falling,
in promise's play.......And the summer to come.
Not only the devotion of these unfolded forces,
not only the paths, not only the evening fields,
not only, after a late storm, the breathing freshness,
not only approaching sleep and a premonition, evenings...
also the nights! Also the high summer nights,
also the stars, the stars of this Earth!

And that natural voice of the human being, like the bird's, would be understood by the whole of a striving nature, from earth to the universe of stars. As the anonymous medieval lyric says, '*Nature comes of love, love to crave*'.

O to be dead at last and know them eternally,
all the stars: for how, how, how to forget them!

And that resonance we feel with nature, with the very stars themselves, is a perception the dead, the wholly transformed, would have, being at one with the whole of the double-realm, and in no way able to forget the beauty of those starry nights.

See, I was calling my lover. But not only she
would come......Girls would come from delicate graves
and gather.....for, how could I limit
the call, once called? The buried always
still seek the Earth. – You, children, a single
thing grasped here is many times valid.

And the wooing call that is at one with Nature is also therefore at one with all the generations of lovers, all the dead as well as the living, all the species. What is grasped once is recapitulated in every childhood.

Don't think that Fate is more than a childhood across:
how often you overtook the beloved, panting,
panting after the blissful chase after nothing, into what's free.

The games of childhood, chasing after nothing, in freedom, are no different than the chase of the beloved after the lover into fulfilment, with here a sexual innuendo of the female overtaking the male in orgasm, as she perhaps still overtakes him in her understanding of love and relationship, man who is *'not at all adequately prepared for love, has not...truly entered into it.'* (Letter, 1912)

Being here is the wonder. You knew it, girls, even you,
you who seemed dispensable, sunken – you, in the worst
streets of the cities, festering, or open
for refuse. Since an hour was given – perhaps not
so much as an hour, one that was scarcely
measurable by time's measure, between two moments, where you
had a being. Everything. Veins filled with being.

And that universal natural wonder of being here, of momentary fulfilment, is open to all of us, even the lowest and most abused. Momentary, transient being, almost out of time, between two moments, can still fill us.

But we forget so easily what our laughing neighbour
neither acknowledges nor envies. We want to visibly
show it, while even the most visible of joys
can only display itself to us when we have changed it, from within.

But we forget such experiences easily, they are individual and inward and therefore opaque to others, and cannot be shown to them, even though we wish to do so, unless we transform the experiences inwardly.

Nowhere, beloved, will world be, but within. Our
life passes in change. And ever-shrinking
the outer diminishes. Where there was once a permanent house,
some conceptual structure springs up, athwart us, as fully
at home among concepts, as if it still stood in the brain.

Life is transience and change, and everything vanishes into thought and memory, into consciousness where things are just as real, but with a different, mental reality, as though the external still stands solid within the internal (or so Rilke claims).

Vast reservoirs of power are created by the spirit of the age,
formless, like the tense yearning gained from all things.
Temples are no longer known. Those extravagances
of the heart we keep, more secretly. Yes, where even one survives,
a single thing once prayed to, served, knelt before –
it stands, as it is, already there in the invisible.
Many no longer see it, but lose the chance to build it
inside themselves now, with columns, and statues, grander!

The spirit of the age, the energy of the universe, now represents a formless reservoir of power, like the tense yearning to create that we acquire from gazing at things, yet is no longer directed into external forms, into the building of the great traditional temples for instance. That energy is now directed internally, to the spaces where we hide their spiritual equivalent within. Whatever spiritual power was possessed by the external forms is still available, though many of us miss the opportunity to rebuild their equivalent inside our conscious minds, greater in form than they once were.

Each vague turn of the world has such disinherited ones,
to whom the former does not, and the next does not yet, belong.
Since even the next is far from mankind. Though
this should not confuse us, but strengthen in us the keeping
of still recognisable forms. This once stood among men,
stood in the midst of fate, the destroyer, stood
in the midst of not-knowing-towards-what, as if it existed, and drew
stars towards itself out of the enshrined heavens. Angel,
I'll show it to you, also, there! It will stand
in your gaze, finally upright, saved at last.
Columns, pylons, the Sphinx, the stirring thrust
of the cathedral, grey, out of a fading or alien city.

The disinherited forms of the past, those charged with spiritual power, such as the columns and pylons of Egyptian temples, and the Sphinx itself, or the thrust of a cathedral spire, say at Chartres, are caught between worlds, between the world of the past where they were created, and the world of the future where they will be lost externally but transformed within us. Nevertheless we should not be confused by this, but determine rather to cherish those forms, which are still recognisable to us. Any one of them was once in the midst of fate, which destroys us, as a part of a previous society's living being, as Being, as if it truly existed in the deep sense, and so brought the universe closer to earth.

Was it not miracle? O, be astonished, Angel, since we are this,
O tell them, O great one, that we could achieve this: my breath
is too slight for this praising. So, after all, we have not
failed to make us of these spaces, these generous ones,
our spaces. (How frighteningly vast they must be,
when they are not overfull of our feelings, after thousands of years.)
But a tower was great, was it not? O Angel, it was though –
even compared to you? Chartres was great – and Music
towered still higher and went beyond us. Why even
a girl in love, oh, alone in the night, at her window,
did she not reach to your knees? –

So that in our small way, we too, created things that have occupied space, created spiritually charged things, built through creative emotion, though time by destroying us, destroying our emotions and feelings, leaves the space available for feeling always unfilled. We, human beings, have created Chartres, that great cathedral, and have given birth to the towering spires of musical composition. And perhaps even woman, the great receptacle of love, might in that love have reached someway towards the heights of the Angel of transformation.

Don't think that I'm wooing.
Angel, were I doing so, you would not come! Since my call
is always full of outpouring: against such a powerful
current you cannot advance. Like an outstretched
arm, my call. And its hand, opened above
for grasping, remains open, before you,
as if for defence and for warning,
wide open, Incomprehensible One.

But the voice that has outgrown wooing, even such a wooing as the bird's pure cry offers with all its resonance, a voice that begins to understand our need for inwardness and inward transformation, should not be misunderstood as wooing the Angel, that agent of transformation which is as yet incomprehensible. Rather the new voice is simply giving, offering, pouring itself out, in a song of lamentation and longing, without calling for response, without offering an entrance to the Angel's reply, such that the Angel could not therefore advance against its current. And the call, like an outstretched hand, palm outward, is wide open as a defence against the Angel and a warning to it, not to destroy the poet yet through an access of transforming energy.

The seventh, and a difficult Elegy has shown that life itself, through resonance with nature and its origins, achieves moments of splendour, but that those moments perish unless they are transformed and taken inward, into our deepest consciousness as individuals and as a species. Just as the great achievements of human beings, the great spiritually-charged buildings, can now only be and must be re-built within us, where modern feeling and spirituality reside, so complex music, and intense love, which express us, need to be retained within our psyche and enshrined in our consciousness. Yet the time is not ripe in the Elegies, which are a song of lamentation we must remember, to fully enter into that transformation or celebrate it, a celebration that would indeed be a song of praise, a song of the double-realms, as the Sonnets to Orpheus are partially intended to be. And the eighth Elegy will return us to lamentation again, to our divided world to gain a still deeper appreciation of our condition. The poet has highlighted previously our transience, distractedness and fear of death, now he looks more closely at consciousness itself.

THE EIGHTH ELEGY

The creature gazes into openness with all
its eyes. But our eyes are
as if they were reversed, and surround it,
everywhere, like barriers against its free passage.

Rilke's *openness* is the eternal and infinite nature of reality, into which the creatures gaze, while we set up barriers against it, and seek to contain the world and grasp it. Rilke writes a number of times about this world of the creatures. '*These, indeed, these confidants of the whole, the animals, who are most at home in a broader segment of consciousness*' he says in 1924. And then in 1926, while referring specifically to this Elegy, '*The animal is in the world, we stand in front of the world.*' Rilke here stresses our discontinuity with the animal realm, whereas the modern position would be to stress continuity through the natural spectrum, including the continuity of mental attributes and consciousness between certain creatures and ourselves. This does not however invalidate Rilke's distinction between more self-conscious human mental processes and normal animal awareness which we currently assume to be less self-conscious and generally directed outwards.

We know what is outside us from the animal's
face alone: since we already turn
the young child round and make it look
backwards at what is settled, not that openness
that is so deep in the animal's vision.

Rilke suggests the child is already focused, by adults, on self-awareness and self-consciousness, and on social habit and acceptable behaviour, so that only by looking at the world of creatures can any of us recognise the external reality in its full depth. Again he discounts the now well-recognised continuity of behaviour between ourselves and other species, and neglects to mention the way creatures lock in to habitual behaviours. Nevertheless, we all recognise the more open contact between wild creatures and their environment, compared with our more artificial created world.

Free from death.
We alone see that:

The creatures, he claims, have no presentiment of their own death: we alone have prescience and foresight, and therefore fear through anticipation. Though this is a questionable statement, certainly regarding the other mammals, it is clear that human awareness of possible futures is greater than in other species.

the free creature
has its progress always behind it,
and God before it, and when it moves, it moves
in eternity, as streams do.

Again he implies that the creature is less aware of past and future than we humans, and moves in the purer moment, free of constraints.

We never have pure space in front of us,
not for a single day, such as flowers open
endlessly into. Always there is world,
and never the Nowhere without the Not: the pure,
unwatched-over, that one breathes and
endlessly knows, without craving.

We live in a state of consciousness where alternatives are always present to us, and identity of space, time and person is established: so that we are always located in a somewhere and are always aware of an elsewhere, and tormented by choice and longing. Thus space and time are impure and qualified, never wholly open and free.

As a child
loses itself sometimes, one with the stillness, and
is jolted back. Or someone dies and is it.
Since near to death one no longer sees death,
and stares ahead, perhaps with the large gaze of the creature.
Lovers are close to it, in wonder, if
the other were not always there closing off the view.....
As if through an oversight it opens out
behind the other......But there is no
way past it, and it turns to world again.

Children, the dying, and the lovers are all closer to the edge of life, to this openness, but the adult world drags back the child from its absorption, while lovers obscure it from each other because their gaze returns to relationship and the human and away from the glimpse of eternity that love offers. That is why unrequited love, Rilke suggested earlier, is nearer to openness, and flows towards infinity rather than falling back always into the world, or mirrors itself and therefore transforms consciousness. Only the dying and the dead are approaching, or are part of, that infinity without self-consciousness, Rilke would maintain.

Always turned towards creation, we see
only a mirroring of freedom
dimmed by us. Or that an animal
mutely, calmly is looking through and through us.
This is what fate means: to be opposite,
and to be that and nothing else, opposite, forever.

We get in the way of the pure flow of Being, and dim the mirror through which we see the world of freedom. The creature's gaze seems to pass through or beyond us (though Rilke's interpretation of that fact is open to debate, since it may simply denote a failure to recognise our expressions, the animals lacking our range of empathetic consciousness). We are the species that stands opposite the infinite, rather than participating wholly in it.

> *If there was consciousness like ours*
> *in the sure creature, that moves towards us*
> *on a different track – it would drag us*
> *round in its wake. But its own being*
> *is boundless, unfathomable, and without a view*
> *of its condition, pure as its outward gaze.*
> *And where we see future it sees everything,*
> *and itself in everything, and is healed for ever.*

A creature that combined a sure animal awareness of openness with a consciousness like ours would disturb our world and drag us along behind it towards the infinite, leading us around as we lead a dog, say. But creatures lack self-consciousness, and live in an endless present, without clear distinction between self and environment. (Again, all very arguable, at least as far as complex species are concerned, though our own greater self-awareness, memory and foresight are not in doubt). Certainly, other species are more at one with their environment than we are with ours, and self-consciousness can indeed seem sometimes like a wound that requires healing.

And yet in the warm waking creature
is the care and burden of a great sadness.
Since it too always has within it what often
overwhelms us — a memory,
as if what one is pursuing now was once
nearer, truer, and joined to us
with infinite tenderness. Here all is distance,
there it was breath. Compared to that first home
the second one seems ambiguous and uncertain.

Yet even the other mammals, like us, sense their distance from the greater security and wholeness of the womb, where the embryonic fluid contained the whole world.

O bliss of little creatures
that stay in the womb that carried them forever:
O joy of the midge that can still leap within,
even when it is wed: since womb is all.
And see the half-assurance of the bird,
almost aware of both from its inception,
as if it were the soul of an Etruscan,
born of a dead man in a space
with his reclining figure as the lid.
And how dismayed anything is that has to fly,
and leave the womb. As if it were
terrified of itself, zig-zagging through the air, as a crack
runs through a cup. As the track
of a bat rends the porcelain of evening.

Rilke wrote in 1914: '*a multitude of creatures that come from externally exposed larvae have that vast vibrant freedom as their womb, how much at home they must feel in it all their lives... this same space conceived them and bore them, and they never have to*

119

leave its security.' He goes on *'in the bird everything becomes more anxious and cautious. The nest that Nature has given it is already a small maternal womb, which it only covers instead of wholly containing.'* Note that the Etruscans depicted the soul as a bird, while a life-sized representation of the dead person adorned their sarcophagus. The bird's nest is a half-womb, like the sarcophagus space with its bird-like soul, and therefore provides only a half-assurance. The flight from the nest is terrifying, like a flight into death, a crack in the cup like a bat's zig-zagging path.

> *And we: onlookers, always, everywhere,*
> *always looking into, never out of, everything.*
> *It fills us. We arrange it. It collapses.*
> *We arrange it again, and collapse ourselves.*

We humans then are always onlookers, voyeurs, watchers of eternity rather than participants, gazers at mirrors rather than participants in the scenes reflected. The world fills our minds and we organise our perceptions, but it is in flux and we cannot hold it still enough to encompass it, though we keep trying, until death empties us again.

> *Who has turned us round like this, so that,*
> *whatever we do, we always have the aspect*
> *of one who leaves? Just as they*
> *will turn, stop, linger, for one last time,*
> *on the last hill, that shows them all their valley - ,*
> *so we live, and are always taking leave.*

We remain separated from reality and so always appear to be leaving it behind as we focus inwards in self-awareness. Our existence is always therefore a kind of departure.

In this eighth Elegy, Rilke has tried to clarify the effects of extreme self-consciousness, and our developed brains, in separating us from the natural world. Even before the effects of our artificial creations, from clothes to cities, our own inner creations of language and thought cut us off from the open infinite world of the creatures, so that we are alienated as well as being distracted, transient, and fearful. In the ninth Elegy, he will seek for some purpose in our human condition that might explain and allow us to transcend our apparent limitations.

THE NINTH ELEGY

Why, if it could begin as laurel, and be spent so,
this space of Being, a little darker than all
the surrounding green, with little waves at the edge
of every leaf (like a breeze's smile) - : why then
have to be human — and shunning destiny
long for destiny?....

W hy be human, asks Rilke, tormented by our fate and longing for
a purpose, when we could be inanimate, if still living (though he
cannot resist personification here, in the breeze's smile — even
the inanimate can seem to mimic humanity), like a laurel? Laurel is of
course used to make the poet's crown since it is sacred to Apollo, god of
the lyre, and it might be better to begin there, as laurel, rather than end as a
laurel-crowned poet.

Oh, not because happiness exists,
that over-hasty profit from imminent loss,
not out of curiosity, or to practice the heart,
which could exist in the laurel......

Happiness (as opposed to joy which Rilke elsewhere celebrates) is not
a justification, since it is a short-term profit from what slips away from us,
our transient lives. Rilke here betrays his and Western Civilisation's endless
longing for permanence and purpose. Transience is a deep problem for
him, though other ways of life, for example Taoism, suggest both
acceptance of transience and immersion in it, encouraging spontaneity, a
merging with natural flows and energies, and the simple delight that
immersion brings. Curiosity is also hardly a motive for enduring this life,
nor the exercise of feeling and emotion since, Rilke posits, that could exist

in some way in the laurel. (He is here unable to resist the image from Ovid of the heart beating under the bark in Ovid's re-telling of the Daphne myth, she being changed into laurel while fleeing Apollo. Note this as a troublesome aspect of Rilke's style, that he will sometimes sacrifice truth, for poetic interest: his response no doubt would have been that Daphne's beating heart still has a psychological reality within the transforming consciousness, only here he is deliberately positing the lapse of such consciousness in favour of existing as laurel instead)

But because being here is much, and because all
that's here seems to need us, the ephemeral, that
strangely concerns us. We: the most ephemeral. Once,
for each thing, only once. Once, and no more. And we too,
once. Never again. But this
once, to have been, though only once,
to have been an earthly thing – seems irrevocable.

Seeking a justification for the human condition, he argues, in a powerful expression of our transience that our presence *seems (scheint)* irrevocable, that all things *apparently* need us, and concern us. The reader should pause here and consider this. *Seems* does not necessarily mean *is*, *apparently* does not necessarily mean *actually* also. Is this more than a mere feeling, more than a subtle form of longing for purpose?

And so we keep pushing on, and trying to achieve it,
trying to contain it in our simple hands,
in the overflowing gaze and the speechless heart.
Trying to become it. Whom to give it to? We would
hold on to it for ever...

Because of this feeling of our necessity despite our transience we keep trying to grasp the world and contain it in our hands, eyes and heart. We try to become the infinite world in order to feel at home, in possession of it. A possession we might give to someone (the beloved, a god?) perhaps, though we wish in fact to keep hold of it forever, even after death.

…Ah, what, alas, do we
take into that other dimension? Not the gazing which we
slowly learned here, and nothing that happened. Nothing.
Suffering then.

But what do we take into the other dimension of death, which is not necessarily afterlife, in Rilke's conception, but simply our transformed consciousness of death? Certainly not our actual gazing or real events (except as memories) both of which are ephemeral; and vanish. Perhaps the record within us of our suffering.

Above all, then, the difficulty,
the long experience of love, then – what is
wholly unsayable.

Do we take there the deep experience of love, which is wholly incapable of expression (as any lover will understand), that which is unsayable?

But later,
among the stars, what use is it: it is better unsayable.

In the dimension of death, or rather the double-realm of wholeness, the suffering, the experience of earthly love is of no use, and is better left unsayable.

Since the traveller does not bring a handful of earth
from mountain-slope to valley, unsayable to others, but only
a word that was won, pure, a yellow and blue
gentian. Are we here, perhaps, for saying: house,
bridge, fountain, gate, jug, fruit-tree, window –
at most: column, tower......but for saying, realise,
oh, for a saying such as the things themselves would never
have profoundly said.

And after all, travellers do not bring unsayable experiences to others, past feelings, like handfuls of meaningless earth that might be anything or have come from anywhere, they bring their recollection of something named and specific, that allows us to realise a landscape or a place or an emotional climate (Rilke is after all an heir of symbolism, himself a symbolist) they bring the name itself, the word. Perhaps we are *here*, rather than in the other realm, in order to carry out that process of saying, a complete saying, a total utterance of things, a deeper saying than the things themselves could hope to 'say' by their pure existence.

Is not the secret intent
of this discreet Earth to draw lovers on,
so that each and every thing is delight within their feeling?
Threshold: what is it for two
lovers to be wearing their own threshold of the ancient door
a little, they too, after the many before them,
and before those to come........, simple.

Is it not Earth's hidden intention to lead lovers on to find every *thing* a delight within their feelings, to transform things into feelings in fact? Threshold is such a thing, such a word...what is it for two lovers to be drawn to wear away their own threshold (of the womb; of sexuality the ancient gateway to delight, to life, to death; of emotion, of relationship, of the sacred temple of love), in the long line of generations...a thing that is simplicity itself?

Here is the age of the sayable: here is its home.
Speak, and be witness.

This is the age for saying *Things*, Rilke claims, because we ourselves through consciousness and language provide a home for the sayable.

More than ever
the things of experience are falling away, since
what ousts and replaces them is an act with no image.
An act, under a crust that will split, as soon as
the business within outgrows it, and limit itself differently.

Moreover this is the age of change, where the ancient things and ways are falling apart, and things are being replaced by processes, processes which will alter as requirements alter, and change their surface manifestations.

Between the hammers, our heart
lives on, as the tongue
between the teeth, that
in spite of them, keeps praising.

And our heart lives on between the hammers that forge these new processes and assail us, as our tongue lives on between the teeth, and continues to praise our being here (poetry being a form of praise, as Rilke reminds us elsewhere).

Praise the world to the Angel, not the unsayable: you
can't impress him with glories of feeling: in the universe,
where he feels more deeply, you are a novice. So show
him a simple thing, fashioned in age after age,
that lives close to hand and in sight.

The Angel, that perfect engine of transformation, is not impressed by the unsayable, since it has already transmuted greater experiences into inward consciousness. But may be amazed by Things, those things we create, that with their continuity and completeness, express life on earth.

Tell him things. He'll be more amazed: as you were,
beside the rope-maker in Rome, or the potter beside the Nile.

Rilke notes, in a letter of 1924, the '*hours I spent in Rome watching a rope-maker, who in his craft repeated one of the oldest gestures in the world – as did the potter in a little village on the Nile.*' He visited Egypt in the winter of 1910-11.

Show him how happy things can be, how guiltless and ours,
how even the cry of grief decides on pure form,
serves as a thing, or dies into a thing: transient,
they look to us for deliverance, we, the most transient of all.
Will us to change them completely, in our invisible hearts,
into – oh, endlessly, into us! Whoever, in the end, we are.

Rilke exhorts us to reveal, to the transforming power, the Things that we create and which surround us, innocent and ours because lacking consciousness but becoming symbols and realities in our consciousness, in memory and in art. Even a cry of grief, a lamentation, can take on form as in these Elegies and become a thing, or merge with a thing, here the created poem. These Things must be transformed endlessly within us into what we are, because they express what we are, and by that creation and transformation we will discover who, in the end, we are, as character, personality, and fate are discovered by living.

Earth, is it not this that you want: to rise
invisibly in us? – Is that not your dream,
to be invisible, one day? – Earth! Invisible!
What is your urgent command if not transformation?

And so, in a paroxysm of personification, and an apotheosis of the sympathetic fallacy, Rilke suggests that Earth itself *desires* its transformation into our invisible consciousness, and to vanish into us, that Earth *commands* us to do this. In the sense that we are partially determined by genetic material and therefore our natural substance, that pre-determination of form at least can *seem* like a command. Rilke goes further, readers must decide if they can follow.

Earth, beloved, I will. O, believe me, you need
no more Spring-times to win me: only one,
ah, one, is already more than my blood can stand.
Namelessly, I have been truly yours, from the first.

Earth, the natural, is also a rightness, and Rilke proclaims himself an adherent not of some artificial other-world, or after-life, not of '*that vilification of earthly life that Christianity has felt obliged to engage in*' as he says in a letter, but of this world and this planet. Again, he says: '*we are set down in life as in the element to which we best correspond.*'

You were always right, and your most sacred inspiration
is that familiar Death.

And Earth's most sacred inspiration is Death, which completes the transient whole, with its permanence, its invitation to us to take our own dead within us and transform them in consciousness, and therefore in a sense take Time itself within us and transform it into eternity. This is a difficult concept, and perhaps an impossible process to even contemplate, and it is hard to understand exactly how Rilke saw death, despite his many pronouncements on it. In a letter of 1923 he came closest perhaps: *'Death is not beyond our strength it is the measuring line on the vessel's brim, and we read 'full' whenever we reach it….I am not saying we should love death, but we should love life so generously, so without calculation and discrimination, that we involuntarily come to include, and to love, death also (the half of life turned away from us)….because we have kept it a stranger it has become our enemy…it is a friend, our deepest friend…and that not in the…sense of life's opposite a denial of life: but our friend precisely when we most passionately and vehemently assent to being here, living and working on Earth, to Nature and love. Life says simultaneously Yes and No. Death (I beg you to believe this!) is the true Yea-sayer. It says only Yes, in the presence of eternity.'* This is Rilke's plea for wholeness, for the acceptance by the transient of our transience, through an acceptance of death, though it is not clear why death cannot be accepted more quietly, as simply the closing of a process, rather than us actively seeking to transform it. Since it is the products of living we absorb, not life's termination specifically, the celebration of death and even of the dead can seem simply morbid, a sickness, unless it is very carefully oriented towards a celebration of life, for example of a dead person's life, and perhaps in a subtle and inward way, in our deep spirits, rather than overtly as a social performance, perhaps the dead should be allowed to find their own place in our consciousness and sub-consciousness, rather than our trying to transform them. However, this is Rilke at his most challenging, throwing down the gauntlet to us, and it is for the reader to decide whether and how far they follow him in this.

*See I live. On what? Neither childhood nor future
grows less……Excess of being
wells up in my heart.*

Rilke proclaims his existence, *I live*. (And so he continues to do in our reading and thinking consciousness, showing that death and life are often linked in the whole) What is it consciousness lives on, what is its food? In this state of hyper-awareness, it lives on everything, all things, the whole, life and death. Childhood and Future of the self (and of the species), the past and the yet-to-be, are not reduced, are not less, are not consumed by our living (even in a temporal sense the past is forever done, finished, complete and eternal, while the future is forever to come, is eternally about to exist as present, so neither can be diminished) both exist in the timeless realm and continue to sustain us, an excess of being, of transformed things, of enriched consciousness, that wells up in the heart, that is beyond transience and is infinite. *Überzählig*, here translated as *Excess*, carries the suggestion of being numerically superior, super-numerous, superfluous to requirements, super-abundant, in excess of even the ability to handle such richness of being.

The ninth Elegy then has suggested our role as transient beings, the celebration and praise of life through taking the things of this world, its external fabric, within us, and there transforming it into a realm of consciousness, making it invisible but still real, so as to enter fully on Being, until Being itself becomes infinite. Note that Rilke does not clearly celebrate other minds here, in relationship, as though relationship was often, despite his claims to wholeness, still beyond him, even though he in turn might claim to have travelled beyond people, in a new relationship with the Angel of transforming consciousness (*'thus I've by-passed people and am now looking cordially back at them'* Letter, 1913) As always, the reader must judge. After this positive endorsement of our role in the ninth, the tenth Elegy, in order to drive home Rilke's message, now attempts to encompass bitterness, pain, grief, sorrow, suffering and death and bring all of the dark side of life into the whole.

THE TENTH ELEGY

Some day, in the emergence from this fierce insight,
let me sing jubilation and praise to assenting Angels.
Let not a single one of the cleanly-struck hammers of my heart
deny me, through a slack, or a doubtful, or
a broken string. Let my streaming face
make me more radiant: let my secret weeping
bear flower.

R ilke's elegiac invocation, reminiscent of Dante's emergence from the Inferno to the light of the stars, anticipates a state of future praise and celebration, in which the fierce insight and understanding (and experience) of suffering involved in the work and the life will finally bear flower, and produce a timeless music. *'I know that one is only entitled to make such full use of the strings of lamentation if one has resolved to play on them, by means of them, later, the whole of that triumphant jubilation that swells up behind everything hard and painfully endured, and without which voices are incomplete'* he wrote in a letter of 1922, on completing the Elegies, regarding these lines above which were written ten years earlier in 1912.

O, how dear you will be to me, then, Nights
of anguish. Inconsolable sisters, why did I not
kneel more to greet you, lose myself more
in your loosened hair? We, squanderers of pain.
How we gaze beyond them into duration's sadness,
to see if they have an end. Though they are nothing but
our winter-suffering foliage, our dark evergreen,
one of the seasons of our inner year — not only
season - : but place, settlement, camp, soil, dwelling.

Our nights of anguish (again, personified) which we gaze past and beyond to see if and when they will end, rather than taking them into us and transforming them, are to Rilke like winter foliage, the dark evergreen face of one of our internal seasons, and in fact not merely a season but the place in which we abide, the space where we exist to suffer transience, loss, pain, that surrounds us like a house, underlies us like the earth, receives us like a place, represents our presence like a settlement.

Strange, though, alas, the streets of Grief-City,
where, in the artificiality of a drowned-out false
stillness, the statue cast from the mould of emptiness bravely
swaggers: the gilded noise, the flawed memorial.

But the city of grief, its social aspect, which these nights of anguish partly preside over, is as Rilke now shows us, a city of darkened vision. Our common handling of grief is to ignore it, conceal it, under the forms of a falsely motionless stage-set, by means of statues of heroes, and prominent people, memorials on which pigeons perch, gilded noisy commemorations, all those market-square methods of formalising grief (though is this not also a transformation of grief into life, into remembrance?)

O, how an Angel would utterly trample their market of solace,
bounded by the Church, bought ready for use:
untouched, disenchanted and shut like the post-office on Sunday.

Religion is targeted as providing a ready-made facile answer to grief and death. '*I reproach all modern religions*', he wrote in a letter of 1923 '*for having provided their adherents with consolation, a glossing over of death, instead of giving them the means of coming to an understanding of it.*' Clearly Rilke suggests the falseness of any idea of a paradisial after-life, or other-world answer to death and mourning, some heavenly realm containing *everything deeply and fervently of the here-and-now* which the Church '*embezzled for the Beyond*' (again a separate Letter of 1923). Rilke despises, as the Angel would, any answer that is bounded by organised religion, already formulated ready for use in some sacred text, rarely part of life, disenchanted with earthly life, and closed off from it like a promise of meaning without enabling our access to it.

Beyond though, the outskirts are always alive with the fair.
Swings of freedom! Divers and jugglers of zeal!
And the figures at the shooting range of easy luck,
targets that shake tinnily whenever some better marksman
hits one. From applause at his luck
he staggers on further: as booths for every taste
are wooing him, drumming, and bawling. Here's something
special, only for adults, to view: how money is got, anatomy,
not just to amuse: the private parts of money,
all of it, the whole thing, the act, - to instruct and make
potent.......

Beyond this formal city though with its churches and temples, on its outskirts, lie commerce and amusements, everything that diverts us from grief, the acrobats and jugglers of the fifth Elegy, the tinny games of chance achievement and fragile status, the eroticism and anatomy of cash which substitutes for true sexuality, the pornography of money that incites greed and ambition.

O, but just beyond
behind the last hoarding, plastered with adverts for 'Deathless',
that bitter beer that tastes sweet to its drinkers,
as long as they chew fresh distractions along with it......
just at the back of the hoardings, just behind them, it's real.

It is even further out, on the furthest edge, behind the hoardings, behind the superficial, plastered with adverts for the bitter promise of an after-life that tastes sweet and intoxicates as long as we don't dwell too much on its implications or possible meaning and reality, behind all that, that we can find *reality*.

Children are playing, lovers are holding each other – to the side,
sombrely, in the sparse grass, and dogs are following their nature.

Children, lovers and creatures, who are all closer to it, closer to reality, infinity, Being than we are, herald a different more natural but barer more sombre terrain, the land of Lament.

The youth is drawn on, further: perhaps it's a young
Lament he loves......He comes to the field, beyond her. She says:
'It's far. We live out there....'
                                            'Where?' And the youth follows.
He is moved by her manner. Her shoulders, her neck – perhaps
she's from a notable family. But he leaves her, turns round,
looks back, waves.......What's the point? She's a Lament.

Here a young Lament, a personification of the early-dead, meets a youth, newly-dead, and directs him onwards to the deeper country of Lamentation. She has nobility, being of ancient and classical stock, descendant of a world more open to grief than ours, more in touch with death and the dead. But he goes on beyond her, turns and looks back as he does so, and waves to her though she is a Lament and so already turned away from almost mortal contact with one still so freshly departed from life.

Only those who died young, in their first state
of timeless equanimity, that of being weaned,
follow her lovingly. She waits
for girls and befriends them. She shows them gently
what she is wearing. Pearls of grief and the fine
veils of suffering. — With youths she walks on
in silence.

Her business is with those who died prematurely, those who are still being weaned away from life, and they are her followers. She takes particular care of young girls who are more attuned to lament (an overtone of the frequent losses to childbirth Rilke encountered? See Requiem), showing them her adornments of grief and suffering, and is silent with young men.

But there, where they live, in the valley, one of the older Laments,
takes to the youth, when he questions: - 'We were,'
she says, 'a large family once, we Laments. Our ancestors
worked the mines on that mountain-range: among men
you'll sometimes find a lump of polished primal grief,
or the lava of frozen rage from some old volcano.
Yes, that came from there. We used to be rich.' —

Further on the newly-dead youth acquires a guide and hears the history of the Laments, how they mined the mountain-range of grief which he will later climb at the end of the Elegy. Rilke suggests our ancestors were superior to us in mining their sorrow, and creating lamentation, and bringing death and suffering into life to enrich consciousness and experience. He is no doubt thinking especially of the Greek myths and tragedies, which he celebrates in various poems, for example his re-enactment of Orpheus' descent to the underworld.

And she leads him gently through the wide landscape of Lament,
shows him the columns of temples, the ruins
of castles, from which the lords of Lament
ruled the land, wisely.

The ancient Greeks perhaps were the lords of Lament, but the Jews' lament over the Babylonian exile, and other elegiac forms may also be in Rilke's mind.

Shows him the tall
Tear-trees, and the fields of flowering Sadness,
(The living know it as only a tender shrub.)
shows him the herds of Grief, grazing – and sometimes
a startled bird, flying low through their upward glance,
will inscribe on the far distance the written form of its lonely cry –

Rilke adds attractive detail to emphasise that we are in the wider country of Lament, which Rilke sees as positive, rather than in the city of Grief and its negative stage-set. Note that the bird's cry is translated by its movement into a tracery of sound across the sky, sound becoming shape, the senses inter-penetrating in this new realm.

At evening she leads him to the graves of the elders
of the race of Laments, the sibyls and prophets.

As suggested above the Greek sibyls and Jewish prophets are archetypes of the elegiac analysis of the human situation and a source of warning.

But as night falls, so they move more softly, and soon,

like a moon, the all-guarding

sepulchre rises. Brother to that of the Nile,

the tall Sphinx, the secret chamber's

countenance.

And they are astonished by the regal head, that forever,

silently, positioned the human face

in the scale of the stars.

Rilke here utilises his experience of Egypt, though this land is '*not to be identified with Egypt, but is only, as it were, a reflection of the Nile-land in the desert clarity of the consciousness of the dead*' (Letter, 1925) The Sphinx here is a *brother* to that at Giza. There is a fine description of the poet's night visit to the Sphinx, in a letter of 1914, where he feels its huge significance as an enduring form in a wasteland, and hears an owl brush the face of the monument, so changing outline into sound, the exact reverse of the process described above when speaking of the bird's cry writing itself on the sky. '*I don't know whether my existence ever emerged so completely into consciousness as during those night hours when it lost all value: for what was it in comparison with all that? The dimension in which it moved had passed into darkness; everything that is world and existence was happening on a higher plane, where a star and a god lingered in silent confrontation.*' Egypt and its numinous statues and temples here express a deeper realm than our everyday one, a region filled with a concentration of spiritual power.

His sight cannot grasp it, still dizzied

by early death. But her gaze

frightens an owl from behind the rim of the crown,

and the bird brushes, with slow skimming flight, along the cheek,

the one with the richer curve,

and inscribes the indescribable

outline, on the new

hearing born out of death, as though

on the doubly-unfolded page of a book.

137

Merely the gaze of the Lament is enough to frighten the owl, bird of wisdom, from behind the rim of the crown. See the passage quoted above for the source of this imagery in Rilke's visit to Egypt. The crown is a *pshent*, the double-crown of the north and south kingdoms, which were united under the later pharaohs, here perhaps symbolising the union of the double-realm of life and death.

And higher: the stars. New stars, of Grief-Land.
Slowly the Lament names them: 'There,
see: the Rider, the Staff, and that larger constellation
they name Fruit-Garland. Then, further, towards the Pole:
the Cradle, the Way, the Burning Book, the Doll, the Window.
But in the southern sky, pure as on
the palm of a sacred hand, the clearly shining M,
that stands for the Mothers......'

Rilke now populates the sky with new constellations, new stars of this land of Grief. This may be a re-naming of real constellations, though the names are too symbolically vague to be assigned. The clearly shining M, suggests the reversed W of Cassiopeia. The names are evocative and mysterious without necessarily suggesting any grand schema. The Rider it has been suggested is the power that directs the horse of human nature, while (Heinrich Cämmerer, 1937) the Staff represents both the harsh cudgel and the pilgrim's staff, the Fruit-Garland ripeness and heaviness, the Cradle birth, the Way life itself, the Burning Book revelation, the Doll the puppet (Puppe) or doll of the fourth Elegy, the Window arrival and parting, or gazing. Rilke's intent if more than simply evocation of mystery is a matter for speculation. The term *Mothers* recalls Goethe's Faust Part II Act I Scene V, see lines 6215 onwards, and their presence as goddesses in the strange realm Faust must visit.

But the dead must go on, and in silence the elder Lament

leads him as far as the ravine,

where the fountain of joy

glistens in moonlight. With awe

she names it saying: 'Among men

this is a load-bearing river.'

Now the youth must go on towards the mountains of grief, which the dead are destined to ascend and visit after life, a metaphor for the understanding of death in the deeper consciousness. At the foot of a ravine, the Fountain of Joy rises, where *fountain* is used here in the sense of a spring, or the source of a river. What is only a stream here is a wide river amongst the living, where it carries us along, supports our burden of pain and suffering by allowing us to release it in a flow of tears and grief. Rilke is here trying to force us to integrate grief into life by paradoxically calling its stream the fountain not of sorrow but of joy (*Freude*). '*Only in joy does creation take place*' (Letter, 1914) '*Whoever does not, sometime or other, give his full and joyous consent to the dreadfulness of life, can never take possession of the unutterable power and abundance of our existence…to show the identity of dreadfulness and bliss…is the true significance and purpose of the Elegies..*'(Letter, 1923) '*For we were this too…When a tree blossoms death as well as life blossoms in it….everywhere around us death is at home, and it watches us out of the cracks in Things*' (Letter, 1915)

They stand at the foot of the mountains.

And there she embraces him, weeping.

He climbs alone, on the mountains of primal grief.

And not once do his footsteps sound from his silent fate.

The newly-dead youth must enter fully into grief, must climb the mountain-range of primal grief, and his fate is silent in this realm.

But if the endlessly dead woke a symbol in us,

see, they would point perhaps to the catkins,

hanging from bare hazels, or

they would intend the rain, falling on dark soil in Spring-time. –

But the dead need to be integrated into our life, says Rilke, and so they might show us a gentler and more earth-bound, mortal, transient image of grief, an image of something that delights and refreshes, not something which is merely morbid, brooding and inimical to us. We humans first think of joy as delight, as something which ascends in us, a rising feeling of exaltation that gazes skywards towards the universe, but the images (implicitly sexual here) of the dangling catkins, symbols of spring, catkins present before the leaves open on the bare hazels, and that of the falling rain, symbolic of a quenching and fertilising flow bringing new life, might re-orient us, and lead us to consider the opposite arc of existence, the other realm which we need to transform within ourselves to be healed and whole, the far-side, the hidden half of our human condition, the other hemisphere of death and grief that complements that of life and delight:

And we, who think of ascending

joy, would feel the emotion,

that almost dismays us,

when a joyful thing falls.

SELECTED FURTHER POEMS
INCLUDING EXCERPTS FROM 'SONNETS TO ORPHEUS'

The Evil Spirits, Auguste Rodin (French, 1840 – 1917).
The National Gallery of Art

LOVE-SONG

How shall I hold my soul so it does not
touch on yours. How shall I lift it
over you to other things?
Ah, willingly I'd store it away
with some lost thing in the dark,
in some strange still place, that
does not tremble when your depths tremble.
But all that touches us, you and me,
takes us, together, like the stroke of a bow,
that draws one chord out of the two strings.
On what instrument are we strung?
And what artist has us in their hand?
O sweet song.

ORPHEUS, EURYDICE, HERMES

That was the strange mine of souls.
As secret ores of silver they passed
like veins through its darkness. Between the roots
blood welled, flowing onwards to Mankind,
and it looked as hard as Porphyry in the darkness.
Otherwise nothing was red.

There were cliffs
and straggling woods. Bridges over voids,
and that great grey blind lake,
that hung above its distant floor
like a rain-filled sky above a landscape.
And between meadows, soft and full of patience,
one path, a pale strip, appeared,
passing by like a long bleached thing.

And down this path they came.

In front the slim man in the blue mantle,
mute and impatient, gazing before him.
His steps ate up the path in huge bites
without chewing: his hands hung,
clumsy and tight, from the falling folds,
and no longer aware of the weightless lyre,
grown into his left side,
like a rose-graft on an olive branch.
And his senses were as if divided:
while his sight ran ahead like a dog,

turned back, came and went again and again,
and waited at the next turn, positioned there –
his hearing was left behind like a scent.
Sometimes it seemed to him as if it reached
as far as the going of those other two,
who ought to be following this complete ascent.

Then once more it was only the repeated sound of his climb
and the breeze in his mantle behind him.
But he told himself that they were still coming:
said it aloud and heard it die away.
They were still coming, but they were two
fearfully light in their passage. If only he might
turn once more (if looking back
were not the ruin of all his work,
that first had to be accomplished), then he must see them,
the quiet pair, mutely following him:

the god of errands and far messages,
the travelling-hood above his shining eyes,
the slender wand held out before his body,
the beating wings at his ankle joints;
and on his left hand, as entrusted: her.

The so-beloved, that out of one lyre
more grief came than from all grieving women:
so that a world of grief arose, in which
all things were there once more: forest and valley,
and road and village, field and stream and creature:
and that around this grief-world, just as
around the other earth, a sun
and a silent star-filled heaven turned,
a grief-heaven with distorted stars –
she was so-loved.

Mercury, Willem Danielsz. van Tetrode (known as Guglielmo Fiammingo)
(Dutch, active Italy, c. 1525 - 1580)
The Los Angeles County Museum of Art

But she went at that god's left hand,
her steps confined by the long grave-cloths,
uncertain, gentle, and without impatience.
She was in herself, like a woman near term,
and did not think of the man, going on ahead,
or the path, climbing upwards towards life.
She was in herself. And her being-dead
filled her with abundance.
As a fruit with sweetness and darkness,
so she was full with her vast death,
that was so new, she comprehended nothing.

She was in a new virginity
and untouchable: her sex was closed
like a young flower at twilight,
and her hands had been weaned so far
from marriage that even the slight god's
endlessly gentle touch, as he led,
hurt her like too great an intimacy.

She was no longer that blonde woman,
sometimes touched on in the poet's songs,
no longer the wide bed's scent and island,
and that man's possession no longer.

She was already loosened like long hair,
given out like fallen rain,
shared out like a hundredfold supply.

She was already root.

And when suddenly
the god stopped her and, with anguish in his cry,
uttered the words: 'He has turned round' –
she comprehended nothing and said softly: 'Who?'

But far off, darkly before the bright exit,
stood someone or other, whose features
were unrecognisable. Who stood and saw
how on the strip of path between meadows,
with mournful look, the god of messages
turned, silently, to follow the figure
already walking back by that same path,
her steps confined by the long grave-cloths,
uncertain, gentle, and without impatience.

ALCESTIS

Suddenly the messenger was there among them,
thrown into the simmer of the wedding-feast
like a new ingredient. The drinkers did not sense
the god's secret entrance, holding his divinity
so close to himself, like a wet mantle,
and seeming one of them, this man or that,
as he passed through. But one of the guests
suddenly saw, in mid-speech, the young bridegroom,
at the table's head, as if snatched up into the heights,
no longer reclining there, and, with his whole being,
mirroring, all over, a strangeness, that spoke to him, with terror.
And immediately after, as though a mixture cleared,
there was silence, only with a residue at the bottom
of clouded noise, and a precipitate
of fallen babbling, already offering the corruption
of musty laughter that has begun to turn.
Suddenly they were aware of the slender god,
and as he stood there, filled inwardly with his mission
and unyielding – they almost knew.
And yet, when it was spoken, it was greater
than all knowledge, none could grasp it.
Admetus has to die. When? This very hour.

But he broke through the shell of his terror
and stretched his hands from the fragments
outwards from them, to bargain with the god.
For years, for only one more year of youth,
for months, for weeks, for a few days,
oh, not days, for nights, for only one,
for one night, for just this one, for this.
The god refused, and then he cried out,
and cried out, and held nothing back, and cried
as his mother cried out in childbirth.
And she appeared near him, an old woman,
and also his father came, his old father
and both stood there, old, worn out, helpless,
by the howling man, who suddenly saw them,
as never before, so close, broke off, swallowed, said:
'Father,
does it matter to you then what's left, the dregs,
that will almost stop you from cramming your food?
Come: pour them away. And you, you, old woman,
Mother,
what are you still doing here: you've given birth?'
And held them both like sacrificial beasts
in his single grasp. All at once he loosed them
and thrust the old people away, filled with an idea,
gleaming, breathing hard, calling: 'Creon! Creon!'
And nothing but that: and nothing but that name.
Yet in his face stood the other name,
he could not say, namelessly expected,
as he held it out, glowing, to his young friend,
that beloved friend, through the table's confusion.
'These old ones (it stood there), you see, are no ransom,
they are used up, and done for, and almost worthless,
but you, you, in all your beauty' –

But then he no longer saw his friend.
He hung back, and that which came, was *her*,
a little smaller almost than he knew her,
and slight, and sorrowful, in her bleached wedding-dress.
All the others are only her narrow path
down which she comes, and comes – (soon she'll be
there in his arms, that have opened in pain)

But as he waits, she speaks: not to him.
She speaks to the god, and the god listens,
and all hear, as it were, within the god:

'No other can be a substitute for him. I *am*.
I am his ransom. For no one else is finished,
as I am. What remains to me then of that
which I was, here? That *is* it, yes, that I'm dying.
Didn't she tell you, Artemis, when she commanded this,
that the bed, that one which waits inside,
belongs to the other world below? I'm really taking leave.
Parting upon parting.
No one who dies takes more. I truly depart,
so that all this, buried beneath him
who is now my husband, melts and dissolves itself –
So take me there: I die indeed for him.

And as the wind changes, over the open sea,
so the god approached as if she were almost one of the dead,
and he was all at once far from her husband,
to whom, concealed in a slight gesture,
he threw the hundred lives of Earth.
He plunged, staggering, towards the two,
and grasped at them as if in dream. They were already
going towards the entrance, into which the women
crowded, sobbing. Once more he still saw
the girl's face, that turned towards him
with a smile, bright as hope,
that was almost a promise: fulfilled,
to come back up from the depths of Death
to him, the Living –

At that, indeed, he threw
his hands over his face, as he knelt there,
so as to see nothing more than that smile.

ARCHAIC TORSO OF APOLLO

We cannot know his undiscovered head
    in which the apples of the eyes ripen. Yet
    his torso still glows like a candelabra,
in which his seeing, now constrained,

remains and shines. Otherwise the curve
of the breast could not dazzle you, nor could a smile
pass through the quiet axis of the loins
to that centre where procreation swelled.

Otherwise this stone would be disfigured, and cut short,
under the shoulders' transparent fall,
and would not glimmer so, like a predator's pelt:

and would not flare out from all its edges
like a star: for here there is no place
that does not see you. You must transmute your life.

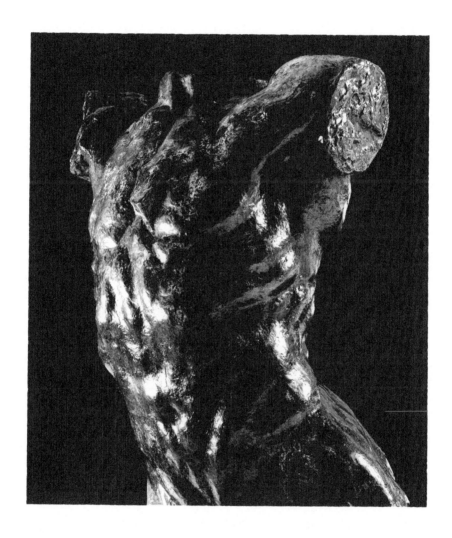

Torso of 'The Falling Man', Auguste Rodin (French, 1840 – 1917)
The Los Angeles County Museum of Art

BUDDHA IN GLORY

Kernel of all kernels, heart of all hearts,
almond, that encloses itself and sweetens –
this universe as far as every star
is your ripening flesh: all hail.

Behold, you feel how nothing more clings to you:
your shell is in the unending,
and there the heavy juice halts and yearns.
And from beyond a brightness helps it,

for all above become your Suns,
full and glowing, turning round you.
But in you is already begun
what will outlast the Suns.

REQUIEM FOR A FRIEND

(Paula Modersohn-Becker 1876-1907)

I have dead ones, and I have let them go,
and was astonished to see them so peaceful,
so quickly at home in being dead, so just,
so other than their reputation. Only you, you turn
back: you brush against me, and go by, you try
to knock against something, so that it resounds
and betrays you. O don't take from me what I
am slowly learning. I'm sure you err
when you deign to be homesick at all
for any Thing. We change them round:
they are not present, we reflect them here
out of our being, as soon as we see them.

I thought you were much further on. It disturbs me
that *you* especially err and return, who have
changed more than any other woman.
That we were frightened when you died, no, that
your harsh death broke in on us darkly,
tearing the until-then from the since-that:
it concerns us: that it become a unique order
is the task we must always be about.
But that even you were frightened, and now too
are in terror, where terror is no longer valid:
that you lose a little of your eternity, my friend,
and that you appear here, where nothing
yet *is*: that you, scattered for the first time,
scattered and split in the universe,
that you did not grasp the rise of events,

as here you grasped every Thing:

that from the cycle that has already received you

the silent gravity of some unrest

pulls you down to measured time –

this often wakes me at night like a thief breaking in.

And if only I might say that you deign to come

out of magnanimity, out of over-fullness,

because so certain, so within yourself,

that you wander about like a child, not anxious

in the face of anything one might do –

but no: you are asking. This enters so

into my bones, and cuts like a saw.

A reproach, which you might offer me, as a ghost,

impose on me, when I withdraw at night,

into my lungs, into the innards,

into the last poor chamber of my heart –

such a reproach would not be as cruel

as this asking is. What do you ask?

 Say, shall I travel? Have you left some Thing

behind somewhere, that torments itself

and yearns for you? Shall I enter a land

you never saw, though it was close to you

like the other side of your senses?

 I will travel its rivers: go ashore

and ask about its ancient customs:

speak to women in their doorways

and watch when they call their children.

I'll note how they wrap the landscape

round them, going about their ancient work

in meadow and field: I'll demand

to be led before their king, and I'll

win their priests with bribes to place me

in front of their most powerful statues,

and leave, and close the temple gates.
Only then when I know enough, will I
simply look at creatures, so that something
of their manner will glide over my limbs:
and I will possess a limited being
in their eyes, which hold me and slowly
release me, calmly, without judgment.
I'll let the gardeners recite many flowers
to me, so that I might bring back
in the fragments of their lovely names
a remnant of their hundred perfumes.
And I'll buy fruits, fruits in which that land
exists once more, as far as the heavens.

    That is what you understood: the ripe fruits.
You placed them in bowls there in front of you
and weighed out their heaviness with pigments.
And so you saw women as fruits too,
and saw the children likewise, driven
from inside into the forms of their being.
And you saw yourself in the end as a fruit,
removed yourself from your clothes, brought
yourself in front of the mirror, allowed yourself
within, as far as your gaze that stayed huge outside
and did not say: 'I am that': no, rather: 'this is.'
So your gaze was finally free of curiosity
and so un-possessive, of such real poverty,
it no longer desired self: was sacred.

    So I'll remember you, as you placed yourself
within the mirror, deep within and far
from all. Why do you appear otherwise?
What do you countermand in yourself? Why
do you want me to believe that in the amber beads
at your throat there was still some heaviness

of that heaviness that never exists in the other-side
calm of paintings: why do you show me
an evil presentiment in your stance:
what do the contours of your body mean,
laid out like the lines on a hand,
so that I no longer see them except as fate?

     Come here, to the candlelight. I'm not afraid
to look on the dead. When they come
they too have the right to hold themselves out
to our gaze, like other Things.

     Come here: we'll be still for a while.
See this rose, close by on my desk:
isn't the light around it precisely as hesitant
as that over you: it too shouldn't be here.
Outside in the garden, unmixed with me,
it should have remained or passed –
now it lives, so: what is my consciousness to it?

     Don't be afraid if I understand now, ah,
it climbs in me: I can do no other,
I must understand, even if I die of it.
Understand, that you are here. I understand.
Just as a blind man understands a Thing,
I feel your fate and do not know its name
Let us grieve together that someone drew you
out of your mirror. Can you still weep?
You cannot. You turned the force and pressure
of your tears into your ripe gaze,
and every juice in you besides
you added into a heavy reality,
that climbed and spun in balance blindly.
Then chance tore at you, a final chance
tore you back from your furthest advance,
back into a world where juices have *will*.

Not tearing you wholly: tore only a piece at first,
but when around this piece, day after day
reality grew, so that it became heavy,
you needed your whole self: you went
and broke yourself, in pieces, out of its control,
painfully, out, because you needed yourself. Then
you lifted yourself out, and dug the still green seeds
out of the night-warmed earth of your heart,
from which your death would rise: yours,
your own death for your own life.
And ate them, the kernels of your death,
like all the others, ate the kernels,
and found an aftertaste of sweetness
you did not expect, found sweetness on the lips,
you: who were already sweet within your senses.

     O let us grieve. Do you know how your blood
hesitated in its unequalled gyre, and reluctantly
returned, when you called it back?
How confused it was to take up once more
the body's narrow circulation: how full of mistrust
and amazement, entering into the placenta,
and suddenly tired by the long way back.
You drove it on: you pushed it along,
you dragged it to the fireplace, as one
drags a herd-animal to the sacrifice:
and still wished that it would be happy too.
And you finally forced it: it was happy
and ran over to you and gave itself up. You thought
because you'd grown used to other rules,
it was only for a while: but
now you were within Time, and Time is long.
And Time runs on, and Time takes away, and Time
is like a relapse in a lengthy illness.

How short your life was, if you compare it
with those hours where you sat and bent
the varied powers of your varied future
silently into the bud of the child,
that was fate once more. O painful task.
O task beyond all strength. You did it
from day to day, you dragged yourself to it,
and drew the lovely weft through the loom,
and used up all the threads in another way.
And finally you still had courage to celebrate.

When it was done, you wanted to be rewarded,
like a child when it has drunk the bittersweet
tea that might perhaps make it well.
So you rewarded yourself: you were still so far
from other people, even then: no one was able
to think through, what gift would please you.
You knew. You sat up in childbed,
and in front of you stood a mirror, that returned
the whole thing to you. This everything was you,
and wholly *before*, and within was only illusion,
the sweet illusion of every woman, who gladly
takes up her jewelry, and combs, and alters her hair.

So you died, as women used to die, you died,
in the old-fashioned way, in the warm house,
the death of women who have given birth, who wish
to shut themselves again and no longer can,
because that darkness, that they have borne,
returns once more, and thrusts, and enters.

Still, shouldn't a wailing of women have been raised?
Where women would have lamented, for gold,
and one could pay for them to howl
through the night, when all becomes silent.
A custom once! We have too few customs.

The Crouching Woman, Auguste Rodin (French, 1840 - 1917)
The Los Angeles County Museum of Art

They all vanish and become disowned.
So you had to come, in death, and, here with me,
retrieve the lament. Can you hear that I lament?
I wish that my voice were a cloth thrown down
over the broken fragments of your death
and pulled about until it were torn to pieces,
and all that I say would have to walk around,
ragged, in that voice, and shiver:
what remains belongs to lament. But now I lament,
not the man who pulled you back out of yourself,
(I don't discover him: he's like everyone)
but I lament all in him: mankind.

      When, somewhere, from deep within me, a sense
of having been a child rises, which I still don't understand,
perhaps the pure being-a-child of my childhood:
I don't wish to understand. I wish to form
an angel from it, without addition,
and wish to hurl him into the front rank
of the screaming angels who remind God.

      Because this suffering's lasted far too long,
and no one can bear it: it's too heavy for us,
this confused suffering of false love,
that builds on limitation, like a custom,
calls itself right and makes profit out of wrong.
Where is the man who has the right of possession?
Who can possess what cannot hold its own self,
what only from time to time catches itself happily,
and throws itself down again, as a child does a ball.
No more than the captain of the ship can grasp
the Nike jutting outwards from the prow
when the secret lightness of her divinity
lifts her suddenly into the bright ocean-wind:
no more can one of us call back the woman

who walks on, no longer seeing us,
along a small strip of her being
as if by a miracle, without disaster:
unless his desire and trade is in crime.

    For *this* is a crime, if anything's a crime:
not to increase the freedom of a Love
with all the freedom we can summon in ourselves.
We have, indeed, when we love, only this one thing:
to loose one another: because holding on to ourselves
comes easily to us, and does not first have to be learned.

    Are you still there? Are you in some corner? –
You understood all of this so well
and used it so well, as you passed through
open to everything, like the dawn of a day.
Women do suffer: love means being alone,
and artists sometimes suspect in their work
that they must transform where they love.
You began both: both are in that
which now fame disfigures, and takes from you.
Oh you were far beyond any fame. You were
barely apparent: you'd withdrawn your beauty
as a man takes down a flag
on the grey morning of a working day,
and wished for nothing, except the long work –
which is unfinished: and yet is not finished.
    If you are still here, if in this darkness
there is still a place where your sensitive spirit
resonates on the shallow waves
of a voice, isolated in the night,
vibrating in the high room's current:
then hear me: help me. See, we can slip back so
unknowingly, out of our forward stride,

into something we didn't intend: find
that we're trapped there as if in dream
and we die there, without waking.
No one is far from it. Anyone who has fired
their blood through work that endures,
may find that they can no longer sustain it
and that it falls according to its weight, worthless.
For somewhere there is an ancient enmity
between life and the great work.
Help me, so that I might see it and know it.

    Come no more. If you can bear it so, be
dead among the dead. The dead are occupied.
But help me like this, so you are not scattered,
as the furthest things sometimes help me: within.

BELOVED

You, lost from the start,
    Beloved, never-achieved,
      I don't know what melodies might please you.
I no longer try, when the future surges up,
to recognise you. All the vast
images in me, in the far off, experienced, landscape,
towns, and towers and bridges and un-
suspected winding ways
and those lands, once growing
tremendous with gods:
rise to meaning in me,
yours, who escape my seeing.

Ah, you were the gardens,
ah, I saw them with such
hope. An open window
in a country house – and you almost appeared,
near me, and pensive. Streets I discovered –
you'd walked straight through them,
and sometimes the mirror in the tradesman's shop
was still dizzy with you and, startled, gave back
my too-sudden image. – Who knows, if the same
bird did not sound there, through us,
yesterday, apart, in the twilight?

FROM SONNETS TO ORPHEUS

I, 1

A tree climbed there. O pure uprising!
O Orpheus sings! O towering tree of hearing!
And all was still. Yet even in that hush
a new beginning, hint, and change, was there.

Creatures of silence pressed from the bright
freed forest, out of lair and nest:
and they so yielded themselves, that not by a ruse,
and not out of fear, were they so quiet in themselves,

but simply through listening. Bellow, shriek, roar
seemed small in their hearts. And where there was
just barely a hut to receive it,

a refuge out of their darkest yearning,
with an entrance whose gatepost trembled –
there you crafted a temple for their hearing.

I, 2

And it was almost a girl, and she came out of
that single blessedness of song and lyre,
and shone clear through her springtime-veil
and made herself a bed inside my hearing.

And slept within me. And her sleep was all:
the trees, each that I admired, those
perceptible distances, the meadows I felt,
and every wonder that concerned my self.

She slept the world. Singing god, how have you
so perfected her that she made no demand
to first be awake? See, she emerged and slept.

Where is her death? O, will you still discover
this theme, before your song consumes itself? –
Where is she falling to, from me?...a girl, almost...

13

Agod can do so. But tell me how a man
is supposed to follow, through the slender lyre?
His mind is riven. No temple of Apollo
stands at the dual crossing of heart-roads.

Song, as you have taught it, is not desire,
not a winning by a still final achievement:
song is being. A simple thing for a god.
But when are we *in being*? And when does *he*

turn the earth and stars towards us?
Young man, this *is* not your having loved, even if
your voice forced open your mouth, then – learn

to forget that you sang out. It fades away.
To sing, in truth, is a different breath.
A breath of nothing. A gust within the god. A wind.

I, 5

Raise no gravestone. Only let the rose
bloom every year to favour him.
Since it is Orpheus. His metamorphosis
in this and that. We don't need

other names. Once and for all
it is Orpheus, when he sings. He comes and goes.
Is it not much already that he sometimes stays
for a few days in the petal of the rose?

O that you understand why he must vanish!
And though he himself is anxious at his vanishing,
while his word surpasses being here,

it's already there, where you can't go.
The lyre-strings don't constrain his hands.
And he obeys, even as he goes beyond.

I, 7

Praising, that's it! As one ordered to praise,
he emerged like the ore from the silent stone.
His heart, O the transient wine-press, among
mankind, of an inexhaustible wine.

When the divine mode grips him
the voice in his mouth never fails.
All becomes vineyard, all becomes grape,
grown riper in his feeling's south.

Neither the must in the tombs of the kings
nor from the gods that a shadow falls,
detracts at all from his praising.

He's a messenger, who always remains,
still holding far through the doors of the dead
a dish with fruit they can praise.

The Prodigal Son, Auguste Rodin (French, 1840 – 1917)
The Los Angeles County Museum of Art

I, 9

Only one who has raised the lyre
already, among the shades,
may sense how to return
the unending praise.

Only one who, with the dead, ate
of the poppy, theirs, from them,
will not lose the slightest
note ever again.

Wish even the image in the pond
that blurs for us, often:
know the reflection.

Only within the double sphere
will the voices become
kind, and eternal.

I, 25

But you now, you whom I knew like a flower
whose name I did not understand,
once more I'll remember, and show them you, stolen one,
beautiful player of the insuppressible cry.

A dancer first, sudden one, body filled with hesitation,
pausing, as if one had cast your young being in bronze:
grieving, listening – Then, from the riches on high,
music fell through your altered heart.

Illness was close to you. Already seized by the shadows,
your blood ran darkly, yet, though suspicious of flight,
it still drove outwards into your natural springtime.

Again and again, broken by darkness and fall,
earthbound, it gleamed. Until after that dreadful pounding,
it stepped through the inconsolable open door.

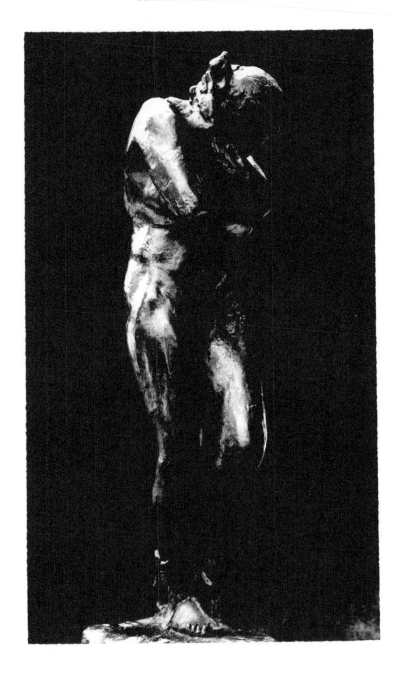

Eve, Auguste Rodin（French, 1840 – 1917）
The Los Angeles County Museum of Art

II, 4

O this is the creature that has never been.
They never knew it and yet none the less
its movements, aspects, slender neck,
up to the still bright gaze, were loved.

True it never *was*, Yet because they loved, it was
a pure creature. They left it room enough.
And in that space, clear and un-peopled,
it raised its head lightly and scarcely needed

being. They didn't nourish it with food,
but only with the possibility of being.
And that gave the creature so much power

that a horn grew from its brow. One horn.
In its whiteness it drew near a virgin girl –
and was in the mirror's silver and in her.

Minotaur or Faun and Nymph, Auguste Rodin (French, 1840 – 1917)
The Los Angeles County Museum of Art

II, 12

Will transformation. O long for the flame,
where a Thing escapes you, splendid in change:
that designing spirit, master of what is earth,
loves only the turning-point in the form's curve,

What closes itself, to endure, already freezes:s
does it feel safe in the refuge of drab grey?
Wait: the hard's warned, by the hardest – from far away,
a blow – the absent hammer is drawing back!

Who pours out like a spring, knowing knows him:
and leads him delighted through the bright creation,
that often ends with the start, and begins with the end.

Every fortunate space is a child or grandchild of parting,
whose passing-through amazes. And Daphne, altered,
since she became laurel, wants you to alter to breeze.

II 13

Be in front of all parting, as though it were already
behind you, like the winter just gone by.
Because among winters is one so endlessly winter
only by over-wintering does your heart still survive.

Be always dead in Eurydice – climb, with more singing,
climb with praising, back to the pure relation.
Here, in the failing place, in the exhausted realm,
be a sounding glass that shattered as it rang.

Be – and know at that time the state of non-being,
the infinite ground of our deepest vibration,
so that you may wholly complete it this one time.

In both the used-up, and the hollow and dumb
recourse of all nature, the un-tellable sum,
joyfully count yourself one, and destroy the number.

II 14

See the flowers, those, so true to the earth,
to whom we lend fate from the margin of fate —
But who knows! If they regret withering
it is for us to be their regret.

All would soar. Only we walk round complaining,
laying down a self from it all, delighted with weight:
O, to Things, what teachers we are, of wearing by taking,
while endless childhood succeeds in them.

Let someone fall into profound slumber, and sleep
deeply with Things — O how easily they'd come
different to a different day, from the mutual deep.

or perhaps remain: and flowers would bloom, and praise
their convert, one now like them
all those mute brothers and sisters, in the winds of the fields.

II, 15

O fountain-mouth, you giver, you Mouth,
inexhaustible speaker of one pure thing –
you, marble mask in the flowing face
of water. And in the land behind

the aqueducts' origins. From further
past graves, from Apennine slopes,
they bring you your speech, that then,
past the darkened age of your chin,

falls, down to the basin below.
This is the sleeping recumbent ear,
the marble ear you always speak to.

An ear of the Earth. She only talks
to herself like this. Place a jug there,
it seems to her that you've interrupted.

II, 28

Oh come and go. You, almost a child still, complete
for a moment the dance-move
into the pure constellation of those dances
in which dull orderly nature's

transiently overcome. Since she was stirred
to total hearing only when Orpheus sang.
You were still moved by those things
and easily surprised if any tree took time

to follow after you into the listening.
You still knew the place where the lyre
lifted, sounding – the un-heard centre.

For it you tried out your lovely steps,
and hoped one day to turn your friend's face
and course towards healing celebration.

II, 29

Quiet friend of many distances, feel
how your breath still enlarges space.
Let yourself ring out, a dark cradled bell
in the timbering. That, which erodes you

gains a strength from your sustenance.
Go out and in, through transformation.
What is your experience of greatest loss?
Is drinking bitter, then become wine.

Be, in this night made of excess,
the magic art at the crossroads of your senses,
the sense of their strange encounter.

And, if the earthbound forget you,
say to the silent Earth : I flow.
To the rushing water say: I am.

WORLD WAS

World was in the face of the beloved –
but suddenly it poured out:
World is outside. World is not to be grasped.

Why did I not drink, as I lifted it,
from the full, the beloved face,
World, so near my mouth scented it?

Ah, I drank. I drank inexhaustibly.
But I was filled up too, by too much
World, and, drinking, I myself overflowed.

STRONGEST STAR

Strongest star that does not need the help
that the night would grant to other stars,
for whom it must first darken, so they may brighten.
Star, already perfect, sink underground,

when the constellations begin their transits
through the slowly-opening night.
Great star, of love's priestesses,
which feeling kindles from itself,

until at last transfigured, never charred,
it sinks down, where the sunlight sank:
surpassing the thousand-fold ascent
with its pure down-going.

His Epitaph

Rose, oh pure contradiction, delight,
of being no-one's sleep under so many
eyelids.

LAMENT

How far it all is,
 And long gone by.
 I believe that star
From which light glitters
Is a million years dead.
I believe, I heard
Something fearful said,
In the boat that floated by.
In the house a clock
Chimed…
In which house?…
I'd like to step out of my heart,
Beneath the vast sky.
I'd like to pray.
And one of all those stars
Must still remain.
I think I know
Which one
Has permanence –
Which one, like a bright city,
Stands, at the end of the sky's radiance.

Head of Sorrow, Auguste Rodin (French, 1840 – 1917)
The Yale University Art Gallery

EVENING

Slowly the evening draws on its coat
    Held out to it by a row of ancient trees:
    You gaze: and the landscape splits in two,
One part lifting skywards, while one falls,

Leaving you not quite part of anything,
Not quite so dark as the house, the silent one,
Not quite as surely invoking the eternal,
As that which turns to star, each night, rising –

Leaving you (indescribably, to unravel)
Your anxious, immense, and ripening life:
So that, now bounded, and now grasped,
It becomes, in turn, stone in you, and star.

THE PANTHER

(In the Jardin des Plantes, Paris)

His gaze is so wearied from the bars
Passing by, that it can hold no more.
It's as if a thousand bars were given him:
And behind the thousand bars, no world.

The soft pace of his powerful, supple stride,
That draws him round in tightened circles,
Is like the dance of force about a centre,
In which a greater will stands paralysed.

Only, at times, the curtain of his pupils
Silently rises – Then an image enters,
Rushes through his tense, arrested limbs,
And echoing, inside his heart, is gone.

THE GAZELLE

(Gazella Dorcas)

Bewitched one: how can two chosen names
Ever achieve the harmony of rhyme
That comes and goes in you, as at a sign.
Out of your brow, branch and lyre climb,

And all you are already, in simile,
Passes through songs of love, whose words,
Soft as rose petals, rest across the eyes
Of one who, no longer reading, closes them.

And sees you: tensed, as if you were
A gun-barrel loaded now with leaps,
But not yet fired, while your neck still

Holds the head, listening: just as when,
Bathing in the woods, a bather attends:
The tree-fringed pool mirrored in her face.

The Kneeling Female Faun, Auguste Rodin (French, 1840 – 1917)
The Los Angeles County Museum of Art

BEFORE SUMMER RAIN

Suddenly from all the parkland's green,
Something, who know's what, is withdrawn:
You feel it coming nearer to the window,
Silently being. Urgently, close and loud,

A plover whistles from the wooded field,
So you'd almost think it a Saint Jerome:
So much of passion and solitude's rising
Out of that single voice, that the rain

Must hear. The walls of the living room,
With all their pictures, move away from us.
They aren't allowed to hear what we say.

And mirrored by the faded tapestries,
Is that uncertain light of afternoon,
Where you are still afraid, like a child.

EARLY PICTURE OF MY FATHER

In the eyes, dream: The brow's in touch
With something far. Vast youthfulness
In the lips, unsmiling seductiveness,
And below the highly ornamented braid
And the slim-chested noble uniform,
The sabre's basket-hilt and both the hands —
Suspended, calm, and clasped on nothing,
And now almost invisible: as if they,
Grasping the distance, were first to vanish.
And all the rest is so self-involved,
So quenched, as if we can't understand it,
And deeply clouded, from its proper depth —

You, swiftly disappearing photograph,
In my more slowly disappearing hand.

SELF-PORTRAIT 1906

Certainty there, in the eyelids' shape,
        Of some ancient, long-ennobled race.
        Childhood's anxious blue still in the eyes,
And here and there, humility, not a fool's
Yet a servant's though, and feminine.
The mouth's, a mouth, large and exact,
Unconvinced, but speaking out for
Justice. The brow's without guile,
Gladly gazing down to quiet shadows.

This, its context's barely suspected:
Neither in adversity nor success
To gather to precise penetration:
Yet serious reality's being planned,
As if with scattered Things, from afar.

TOMBS OF THE COURTESANS

There they lie, in their long hair,
    Brown faces sunk deep in themselves.
    Eyes as if fronted by too vast a distance.
Skeletons, mouths, flowers. In the mouths
Gleaming teeth like travelling chessmen
Set out there in their ivory rows.
And flowers, yellow pearls, slender bones,
Hands and tunics, shrivelled fabric,
Over decayed hearts. But there,
Below those rings, those talismans,
And jewels blue as eyes (lovers' gifts)
The silent crypt of sex remains,
Filled to its arch with flower-petals.
And more yellow pearls, rolled about –
Bowls of fired clay, whose curves
Affect their portraits, green shards
Of ointment-jars, smelling of flowers,
And forms of little gods: household altars.
Courtesan-heaven, with delighted gods.
Broken belts, and shallow scarabs,
Tiny figures with vast genitals,
A smiling mouth, dancers and runners,
Golden clasps like little hunting bows,
Chasing after bird and beast amulets:
Long needles, decorated cutlery,
And a potsherd with a reddened ground,
Where like a dark inscription on an arch,
A four-horse chariot team's limbs stiffen.

The Sirens, Auguste Rodin (French, 1840 - 1917)
The National Gallery of Art

And more flowers, pearls, rolled apart,
The gleaming sides of a little lyre,
And, between the veils like falls of mist,
As if it crept from the shoe's chrysalis,
The delicate butterfly of the ankle.

So they lie filled with Things,
Costly Things, gems, utensils, toys,
Smashed trinkets (how much fell into them!)
And they darken like a river-bed.

They *were* riverbeds,
Over them, in brief swift waves
(Willing themselves on to further life)
The bodies of countless youngsters plunged,
And the streams of grown men roared.
And sometimes boys, breaking from the hills
Of childhood, flowed in timid falls,
And played with sunken Things,
Until the slope captured all feeling,

Then filled with clear shallow water
The whole breadth of the broad canal,
And stirred its whirlpools in the depths,
Mirroring the banks for the first time,
And far-off birdsong – while in the sky
The starry nights of a sweeter land
Opened on high, and would never close.

THE SPIRIT ARIEL

(On Reading Shakespeare's Tempest)

Sometime, somewhere, you had set him free
With a jolt, with which we tear ourselves away
From youth, to greatness: from all consideration.
Then, he was willing: and since then he's served,
Impatient, after every task, for freedom.
And half imperiously, half almost ashamed,
You put it to him you've still need of him,
For this and that, ah, and must tell him
How you helped him. And yet you feel yourself
That all that's held back here, with him,
Is missing from the air. So tempting, sweet,
To let him go – and then, there's no more magic:
Committing yourself to Fate like all the others,
Knowing that his weightless friendship,
Lacking strain, with no more obligation,
An excess of the space you breathe,
Works on, without thought, in the Element.
Dependent now, and no longer gifted
With shaping your dull mouth to the call
At which he dived. Powerless, ageing, poor,
Yet breathing *him*, like an incomprehensible
Far-flung fragrance, that makes the unseen
Complete. Smiling that you once could so
Summon him, used so easily to such
Great undertakings. Perhaps weeping too,
Remembering how he loved, and wished
To leave you, always both at once.

(Have I loosed him, already? This man, become
A duke again, terrifies me. How gently
He draws the wire through his head
And hangs himself beside the other
Figures, and brings forward his speech
And asks for mercy…What an epilogue,
Of consummate power. Throwing off, standing
Naked, with only one's strength: 'which is most faint'.)

Vast Night

I was often amazed by you, stood at the window begun
Yesterday, stood and was amazed. As yet the new
City was denied me, and the un-persuadable landscape
Darkened as though I were nothing. The nearest Things
Didn't care if I understood them. And the street
Pressed on the lantern: I saw it was alien.
Over there – a room, sensed, clear in the lamplight.
Already I took part: they knew, closing the shutters.
Stood. And a child cried. I knew what the mothers
All around, in the houses, could do – and knew
As well the inconsolable root of all tears.
Or a voice sang out, and reached a little beyond
Expectation, or an old man below coughed
Full of reproach, as though his body was right
To oppose the gentler world. Then an hour struck –
But I began counting too late, and it fell past me –
Like a child, a stranger, finally allowed to play,
Who can't catch the ball, no good at games
That the others all indulge in so deftly,
Stands there and stares – at what? Standing there, I
Suddenly grasped it was *you* surrounding me, playing,
Grown-up Night, and I wondered at you. Where towers
Raged, where, turned away from Fate, a city
Enclosed me, and un-guessed at mountains
Piled up against me, and strangeness, in narrowing
Circles, prowled around my random flickers
Of feeling – It was then, great one,
Unashamed yourself, that you knew me. Your breath

Passed over me. Your smile spreading across
Solemn distances, entered me.

TURN OF THE ROAD

(The path from inwardness to greatness
Passes through sacrifice.   - Kassner.)

For ages he gained it by watching.
　　Stars fell to their knees
　　　Beneath his struggling gaze.
Or he watched, kneeling,
And his urgency's fragrance
Made some god so weary
It smiled at him in its sleep.

Towers he looked at so
They were startled:
Building them again, suddenly in an instant!
But how often the landscape
Over-freighted by day,
Was brought to rest, at dusk, in his silent awareness.

Creatures trusted him, wandering
Into his open gaze, grazing,
And the caged lions
Stared as if at ungraspable freedom:
Birds flew bravely
Straight through it: flowers
Gazed endlessly into it
Immense, as in childhood.

And the rumour a watcher existed
Moved the less,
More doubtfully, visible,
Moved the women.
Watching for how long?
How long now, inwardly deprived,
Beseeching, from the depths of his look?

When he, one who waits, sat there in alien space:
The hotel's distracted, un-noticing room,
Sullen, around him, and in the evaded mirror
The room again
And later, from the tormenting bed,
Again:
There in the air, considered,
Inconceivably considered
His perceivable heart
His through-the-painfully-buried body
Still perceivable heart
Considered and judged:
That it had no love.

(And refused him further communion)

For there's a limit to gazing.
And the gazed-at world
Wants to blossom in love.

The work of vision is done,
Now do heart-work
On the forms in you that you've caught: since you've
Overpowered them: but still don't know them.
Inner man, look on your inner woman,

Suzon, Auguste Rodin (French, 1840 – 1917)
The Los Angeles County Museum of Art

The creature that's won
From a thousand natures, the one
Gained just now, but not
Yet, truly, loved.

HEART-SLOPES

Out on the heart-slopes. See, how tiny down there,
See, the last village of words, and higher,
But how little still, one last
Farmhouse of feeling. Do you know it?
Out on the heart-slopes. Stone ground
Under the hands. Something still
Grows here: on a dumb ledge,
An unknowing plant blooms, sings out.
And the knower? Ah, who began to know
And is silent now, out on the heart-slopes.
There fully conscious many a mountain
Creature, sure-footed, lingers,
Passes. And a huge bird securely
Circles the pure peak of denial – But
Insecure, here on the slopes of the heart...

SPACE

What birds fall through is not customary
  Space, where forms increase for you.
  (Out there, you'd be denied yourself
And you would disappear, without a trace.)

Space reaches out of us, and translates Things:
For a tree's Being to succeed for you
Throw inner space around it, from that space
You know inside yourself, surround it with constraint.
It has no boundaries. Not till it's formed
By your renunciation is it ever truly 'tree'.

PALM

Hand's inwardness. Sole, that no longer walks
Except by feeling. That holds itself out
And in its mirror receives
Celestial roads, that wander
Along themselves:
That has learned to walk on water
When it scoops:
That travels from fountains
Transforming every path:
That steps into other hands,
Making a landscape
Of those that resemble it,
Wanders and enters them,
Filling them full of arrival.

Left Hand of Pierre de Wissant, Auguste Rodin (French, 1840–1917)
The Los Angeles County Musuem of Art

ALWAYS AGAIN

Always again, though knowing love's landscape,
And the tiny churchyard of plaintive names,
And the ravine where others end, where terrible
Silence reigns – always again we go out, together,
Under the ancient trees, always again we lie,
Among flowers, face to face with the sky.

ENDURE

Are not Nights formed out of the painful space
Of all the embraces a lover suddenly loses?
Eternal beloved, you who wish to endure: give
Yourself out like a fount, enclose yourself like laurel.

WAITING

Beside the sun-drenched roadway,
In the cleft tree's hollow, a trough,
So long, whose dripping surface
Quickly renews, I'll quench my
Thirst: the source and play of water
Penetrates right through my wrists.
Drinking would seem too much to me,
Too clear: But this gesture brings
Glittering water to consciousness.

So, if you came to me I'd need, to sate me,
Only the lightest touch of my two hands
Over the fresh young curve of your shoulders,
Over the swelling of your breasts.

PRAISE

O tell me Poet what you do? – I praise.
But the deathly and the monstrous,
How do you accept them, bear them? – I praise.
But the nameless, the anonymous.
How, Poet, can you still invoke it? – I praise.
Under every costume, every mask of us,
What right have you to be true? – I praise.
Or that the calm and the impetuous
Should know you, as star and storm? – Because I praise.

ELEGY

(To Marina Tsvetayeva)

Oh the losses in All, Marina, the falling stars!
    We can't add to it, wherever we hurl ourselves
        To whatever star! All is already a part of the whole.
So even when we fall, the sacred sum's not lessened.
Whoever's given to feeling falls to the source and is healed.
Is it all a game, equal exchange, displacement,
Nowhere a name, nowhere natural achievement?
Waves, Marina, we're sea! Depths, Marina, we're sky.
Earth, Marina, we're earth, a thousand times Spring,
Like larks an outpouring of song hurls to the unseen.
We begin as joy: it already utterly exceeds us:
Suddenly our weight bows the song down to lament.
But then: lament? Isn't that a younger, deeper joy.
Even the gods of the deep wish to be praised, Marina.
Gods are so innocent they wait for praise like children.
Praising, dear one, let's be generous with praise.
Nothing is ours. We set our hands lightly on the necks
Of unbroken flowers. I saw it at Kom Ombo, on the Nile:
Thus, Marina, those kings offered up gifts they renounced.
As angels mark the doors of those to be saved,
We touch this and that, seemingly tender.
Ah how far off already, ah how careless, Marina,
Even in our innermost pretences. Signposts that's all.
This gentle commerce, when it no longer suffers
One of our kind, seizes them in its grasp, takes
Its revenge and kills. That it has power to kill
Was clear to all from its delicacy and restraint

And from the strange force that alters us
From living ones to survivors. Non-being. Do you
Remember how often blind command dragged us
Through the icy ante-room of birth…Dragged: *us*? A body
With eyes under countless eyelids, refusing. Dragged
That heart, a whole race, set down in us. Dragged
To the goal of migratory birds the flock, the form of our
Imminent change. Lovers, Marina, weren't, are not
Permitted to know utter destruction. Must be as if new.
Only their grave is old, only their grave remembers,
Darkens under the sobbing tree, remembers it all.
Only their grave sinks: they are supple as reeds:
What bends them too far, weaves them richly in garlands.
How they flower on May winds! From the midst of Ever,
Where you breathe and sense, the instant shuts them out.
(O how I comprehend you, feminine flower on the same
Undying stalk. How strongly I scatter myself
Into the night air that will soon reach you) The gods
Long ago learnt how to simulate halves. We drawn into
That orbit filled ourselves out like the orb of the moon.
Even in times of waning, even in weeks of change
Nothing could ever again help us to richness, but our
Own solitary passage over the unsleeping landscape.

THE DOVE

(To Erika, for the Festival of Praise)

Far from the dovecote the dove that remains outside,
Finding its home again one with the day and night,
Knows real serenity since all its deepest fright's
Touched by relatedness throughout its furthest flight.

Those doves below, the ones utterly cared for,
Never-endangered ones cannot know tenderness:
Hearts that are won again are the most lived-for:
Free through renouncing joyful in skilfulness.

Over all Non-being arches the Everywhere!
Ah now the far-flung ball, thrown if we truly dare,
Doesn't it fill our hands returning, otherwise:
Weighted by homecoming more the prize.

INDEX OF POEMS BY FIRST LINE

NOTES

Gaspara Stampa. *1523-1554. Famous for her intense love for the young Lord of Treviso, Collaltino, which he was ultimately unable to return. She wrote some two hundred sonnets telling the story of her love for him, dying at the age of thirty-one. She was for Rilke a 'type' of unrequited love.*

Santa Maria Formosa. *The church, in Venice, which Rilke visited in 1911. The reference is to one of the commemorative tablets, inscribed with Latin texts, on the church walls.*

Linos. *The mythical poet: in some versions of Greek myth, he is the brother of Orpheus, and son of Calliope the Muse. The ancient 'Lament for Linos' was part of the vegetation rituals mentioned by Homer (Iliad XVIII, 570). The Greek myths provide a complex of hints about him, that involve, song and music, ritual lament, and the sacred nature of poetry.*

Tobias. *The Book of Tobit in the Apocrypha (5:4,16) tells the story of Tobit the Israelite, who ordered his son Tobias to go and recover some of his property from Media. The Archangel Raphael, disguised, guided the young man. 'So they went forth, and the young man's dog with them.'*

The boy *with the brown squinting eyes. Rilke's cousin, Egon von Rilke, who died in childhood. His brown eyes were 'disfigured by a squint'.*

Les Saltimbanques. *This elegy is founded on Rilke's knowledge of Picasso's painting Les Saltimbanques (he lived, from June to October 1915, in the house where the original hung, in Munich). Picasso depicts a family of travelling acrobats. Rilke was familiar with such people from his stay in Paris, where he became Rodin's secretary.*

RAINER MARIA RILKE

Rainer Maria Rilke, was born in Prague, the capital of Bohemia, then part of Austria-Hungary now the Czech Republic, in 1875. He studied in Prague and Munich, later travelling to Italy, Russia (where he became acquainted with Boris Pasternak's family) and Germany where he met and married Clara Westhoff. Their daughter Ruth was born in 1901. In 1902 he travelled to Paris, where he subsequently became Rodin's secretary, and where under Rodin's influence he developed the more objective style of his collection *New Poems* (*Neue Gedichte, 1907*).

Rilke also spent time in Spain, at Ronda. In 1911 and 1912 he was at Duino, near Trieste, where he began the *Duino Elegies*, but spent the years of the First World War in Munich, before moving to Switzerland in 1919. He finally settled at Muzot, near Sierre in the Valais, where in a burst of inspiration, in 1921 and 1922, he completed the *Duino Elegies* and wrote the *Sonnets to Orpheus*. He produced a substantial number of further individual poems, which expressed his mature thought. After long periods of illness, he died at a sanatorium near Montreux in December 1926.

The *Duino Elegies* and *Sonnets to Orpheus* deploy and extend both his early lyrical gifts and subsequently more objective formal style in a poetry of philosophical and spiritual depth, centred around a view of life and death as forming a complete whole, and demanding a full human response to both the positive and negative aspects of both these 'realms'. In that sense he is a poet of both darkness and light, of the bleak and sparse but also the spiritual and consolatory. Ideas from late nineteenth century existentialist philosophy, the influence of artists like Rodin and Picasso, and a subtle awareness of Psychology as a developing area of intellectual exploration, can all be found in his work, while his spiritual and poetic world is revealed as both highly individualistic and profoundly modernistic, despite its Romantic lyrical heritage.

About the Translator & Commentator

Anthony Kline lives in England. He graduated in Mathematics from the University of Manchester, and was Chief Information Officer (Systems Director) of a large UK Company, before dedicating himself to his literary work and interests. He was born in 1947. His work consists of translations of poetry; critical works, biographical history with poetry as a central theme; and his own original poetry. He has translated into English from Latin, Ancient Greek, Classical Chinese and the European languages. He also maintains a deep interest in developments in Mathematics and the Sciences.

He continues to write predominantly for the Internet, making all works available in download format, with an added focus on the rapidly developing area of electronic books. His most extensive works are complete translations of Ovid's Metamorphoses and Dante's Divine Comedy.

Printed in Great Britain
by Amazon

56123059R00129